Beyond the Beginning

A Reader in English

D0140377

Keesia Harrison Hyzer
Madison Metropolitan School District
Madison, Wisconsin

Ann Marie Niedermeier
Madison Metropolitan School District
University of Wisconsin
Madison, Wisconsin

Mary Mitchell Church
Madison Metropolitan School District
Madison, Wisconsin

PRENTICE HALL REGENTS
Englewood Cliffs, New Jersey 07632

Library of Congress Cataloging-in-Publication Data

Hyzer, Keesia Harrison.
  Beyond the beginning : A Reader in English / Keesia Harrison Hyzer, Ann
Marie Niedermeier, Mary Mitchell Church : illustrated by Emily Church.
  ISBN 0-13-068164-4
  1. English language—Textbooks for foreign speakers.
2. Readers—1950–   I. Niedermeier, Ann Marie.   II. Church, Mary
Mitchell.   III. Title.
  PE1128.H89   1991
  428.6'4—dc20

                                                          89-72100
                                                          CIP

Editorial/production supervision and
  interior design: Kala Dwarakanath
Cover design: Diane Conner and Marianne Frasco
Manufacturing buyer: Ray Keating
Illustrations: Emily Church

© 1991 by Prentice-Hall, Inc.
A Division of Simon & Schuster
Englewood Cliffs, New Jersey 07632

Printed in the United States of America
10 9 8 7 6 5 4 3 2 1

ISBN 0-13-068164-4

Prentice-Hall International (UK) Limited, *London*
Prentice-Hall of Australia Pty. Limited, *Sydney*
Prentice-Hall Canada Inc., *Toronto*
Prentice-Hall Hispanoamericana, S.A., *Mexico*
Prentice-Hall of India Private Limited, *New Delhi*
Prentice-Hall of Japan, Inc., *Tokyo*
Simon & Schuster Asia Pte. Ltd., *Singapore*
Editora Prentice-Hall do Brasil, Ltda., *Rio de Janeiro*

Contents

Newspaper Reading

Preface

Beyond the Beginning: A Reader in English is a comprehensive reading book for secondary and adult students of English as a second language at the intermediate level. In this text, the authors have taken recent advances in theory and put them into practice. The text focuses on reading as a process, with comprehension enhanced by exercises in all skill areas. The chapters are designed to provide students with a variety of reading experiences which will broaden their knowledge of the world and improve their reading skills while they learn to enjoy reading. The readings are organized into three sections: fiction and poetry; fact; and newspaper reading.

All of the reading passages and exercises have been developed through intensive field testing with secondary and adult learners. In the fiction and poetry section there are stories of universal appeal, like myths and folktales, as well as some "to be continued" stories which encourage students to predict the story endings. The chapter which introduces poetry does not require that the student or teacher have previous experience with poetry. The factual reading section includes heartwarming human interest stories and a selection about the immigrant experience. The selections in the newspaper reading section motivate students to learn about the world around them through newspapers. Although the chapters increase in difficulty as the text progresses, each chapter is self-contained so that teachers can arrange their syllabus according to the needs and interests of their students.

In this text, reading is an interactive process that includes prereading, reading, follow-up, and the opportunity for more reading practice through the selections at the end of each chapter. Prereading exercises enable students to organize, plan, and gain the knowledge necessary for the reading experience. Each reading passage helps students expand their communicative vocabulary and world knowledge. The follow-up exercises (listening, speaking, and writing) are integrated with the readings. A skills section and suggestions for extra reading help students stretch their abilities, transfer reading skills, and grow to be mature readers. With this text, students can improve their English language skills by developing independence in reading and strengthening their listening, speaking, and writing abilities. Grammar and vocabulary are controlled, but students are exposed to rich and varied language used in real-life situations.

A large number of exercises, varied in both type and level of difficulty, have been included so that teachers can select from them according to the needs of their classes. All teachers will not use all exercises; however, we encourage teachers to try exercises that at first seem difficult. Field testing has shown that they are successful with students of very limited educational backgrounds, especially when in-class modeling precedes assigning the more independent tasks. Many of the exercises are designed for group work, emphasizing the communicative nature of language and helping students at different skill levels learn together and build independence from the teacher. These exercises have been constructed to follow principles of cooperative learning; there is built-in interdependence, and the role of each student in the group is important. Teachers will want to emphasize necessary social skills to help students participate fully in a communicative and cooperative classroom.

The authors have avoided including specific assessment tools in this text. Due to a wide variety in program organizations, teaching styles, and students' own educational and cultural backgrounds, teachers can best determine their own assessment criteria and goals. When using this interactive text, teachers will want to assess student progress in all language skills—listening, speaking, reading, and writing.

Teaching Suggestions

During prereading, students get ready to read by exploring the general topic of the chapter. The illustrations are an integral part of the prereading experience, helping students visualize and comprehend the chapter topic. The prereading questions stimulate classroom discussion so that students can share and build on existing knowledge for later comprehension. These prereading exercises help the teacher find out what students already know, and what they need to know in order to comprehend successfully. Students gain motivation and purpose to read. The questions encourage students to organize for and predict about the reading passage.

The vocabulary that students need for the reading passage is included in the prereading section, and there is an additional vocabulary exercise after the reading. Teachers might choose to do several vocabulary exercises before the reading, or save most vocabulary work for afterwards, depending on the students' basic knowledge about the topic of each chapter. The vocabulary exercises encourage students to guess at meanings and use context clues, thereby becoming more independent in their reading skills and linking vocabulary to text rather than to word lists. Students learn vocabulary by using words frequently in listening, speaking, reading, and writing, so vocabulary growth occurs as words are recycled in various exercises in each chapter. Teachers may also want to use word games, such as Bingo or Concentration, to reinforce vocabulary.

The reading passage should first be presented in its entirety. Students benefit from hearing the teacher read the whole passage to them as they follow along, reading silently. Having the students read the text silently, aloud, or in role-play offers additional exposure to and practice with the text. The teacher may also take the opportunity to model comprehension strategies for students, thereby teaching reading skills in context. The comprehension section following the reading passage includes some questions that require factual answers and others that are more challenging.

The listening and conversation sections encourage the expansion of vocabulary and ideas related to the chapter topic. For some listening exercises, the students will be directed to close their books. They listen as the teacher reads varied types of short texts, and then they answer basic questions about these texts. The conversation section is interactive. Teachers are urged to have students work in pairs and small groups whenever possible to develop communicative skills.

The skill builder section focuses on entry-level academic or practical skills. Students are to be encouraged to practice and apply these skills in many contexts, and cumulatively practice them as they proceed through the text. This skill section helps students grow toward reading sophistication.

The writing section, designed to help students think about and explore the chapter topic, is often closely linked to the previous exercises in the chapter. These exercises serve as preparation for writing. The focus in the writing section should be on expressing ideas through writing rather than on accuracy of grammar, punctuation, and so forth. Students are often asked to share their writing with classmates, thereby stimulating more discussion and thinking about the chapter topic. Teachers may wish to model writing passages with the whole group before asking for individual production, especially when beginning to use the text.

In the section dealing with more reading, students will find additional reading tasks in varied forms to be read in a less intensive way. These readings, building on a topic already well explored in the first reading passage and exercises, lead students to independent reading behavior. The extras section serves as a time-saving resource for students and teachers. Students might be motivated to find a reference on a topic which particularly interests them, or teachers might read short selections from the resource list aloud each day. Many of the books contain pictures which help explain the topic at hand or stimulate conversation and questions. Video suggestions are also included and could be used for in-class or at-home viewing.

Many of the exercises and activities in each chapter can be assigned as homework. Students will profit from reading, oral, and written assignments. The following are suggestions for homework in each chapter section.

Prereading:	Guess the meanings of vocabulary words in "What does it mean?"
	Write questions the story might answer.
Reading:	Reread the story.
	Prepare to read orally.
	Prepare for cloze or dictation exercises.
Comprehension:	Write the answers to the questions.

Vocabulary:	Write sentences using the vocabulary words.
Listening:	Listen to related news or TV programs.
Conversation:	Read the directions to prepare for the conversation activities. Take notes.
Writing and Skill Builder:	Write the answers to the exercises at home after talking about them in class.
More Reading:	Read the story at home after discussing the vocabulary. Write the answers to the questions.

1

The Shadow

Prereading

A. What do you think?

1. What is a mystery story?
2. Look at the picture and make guesses about the mystery story *The Shadow*.

B. What does it mean? Read the following sentences. What do the underlined words mean?

1. I didn't <u>realize</u> you were unhappy. I thought you liked school.
2. Some people have bad eyesight and they cannot see <u>clearly</u>.
3. When the sun shines, you can see the <u>shadows</u> of trees on the ground.
4. He was so scared he was <u>shaking</u>. He couldn't keep his hands quiet.
5. Flying in an airplane makes me feel <u>anxious</u>. I get very nervous.

Reading

THE SHADOW

Something strange was going on, and Kim felt very anxious. Every time she went out, she saw the same person on the street. After a while she realized that this person was watching her.

It was a man—a tall, thin man who always walked fast and silently. He wore a large coat and a hat pulled down over his face so Kim never saw him clearly. He was like a shadow—always near her, but not quite real.

She tried to think back, to remember where she first saw him. Was it on the bus on her way to work? Was it in the halls at night school? Maybe it was outside on the sidewalk in front of her apartment building. She didn't know, but she was beginning to have nightmares about him. Sometimes at night she woke up shaking, and once she ran to the bedroom window to see if anybody was there.

Now she worried about this stranger all the time. She had trouble studying and working. She made mistakes and forgot things. When she looked in the mirror, she saw big circles under her eyes, and she looked afraid. Maybe she was going crazy. Why was this happening to her? Who was this man? What did he want?

To be continued . . .

Exercises

Comprehension

C. Answer the following questions.

1. Why was Kim feeling anxious?
2. What do you know about the person who followed Kim?
3. Why was the man like a shadow?
4. Where and when did Kim first see the man?
5. Name three problems Kim had because of the man.
   Example: *She had nightmares*.
   (a)
   (b)
   (c)

D. Why was the man following Kim? With your classmates, make a list of your ideas and discuss them. Later you will write your own ending for the story.

Vocabulary

E. For each word, write an antonym (a word that means the *opposite*) in the blank.
Example: fast _____ *slow* _____

1. silently _____
2. close (adjective) _____
3. thin _____
4. forget _____
5. strange _____
6. anxious _____

Listening

F. **Books closed.** Listen to the following description of a house. You will hear it two times. Take notes as you listen, and then draw a picture of the house. Discuss the following words and phrases before you begin.

to need repair	narrow
in bad shape	chimney
stories (tall)	

The huge, old wooden house was three stories tall. It had a high, narrow roof. A low, broken fence circled the house and yard. The yard looked very bad; three trees had fallen down, and the grass was not cut. The house was in bad shape, too. Most of the windows were broken, and the front steps needed repair.

But the house *was* being used. A family of birds had made their home on top of the chimney, and some squirrels came in and out through the open front door to look for food.

Now open your books and read the description to see if your drawing is correct. Compare drawings with a partner.

G. Agree/Disagree. You will hear five statements about living in an American city. If you agree, write *A*. If you disagree, write *D*. Then discuss your answers with the class.

_____ 1. In this city, it's not dangerous to walk alone at night.
_____ 2. It's not important to lock your car if you are shopping in the daytime.
_____ 3. The U.S. is not a dangerous place to live. I feel safe here.
_____ 4. You should tell children never to speak to strangers.
_____ 5. Young women shouldn't live alone. It's too dangerous.

Conversation

H. Think about a scary story that you know. It can be a true story that someone told you, a dream, or a famous story. Write a few words about what happens first, second, third, and so on. Then use these notes to tell the story to the class.

Writing

I. Work in pairs and write an ending for the story "The Shadow." Your ending should be one paragraph long. Use one of the ideas from the list in exercise D, or use one of the following sentences to start your paragraph. When you finish, read your paragraph aloud to your partner or classmates.

1. One day, the man came up to Kim and said, ". . .
2. One night around midnight, Kim heard footsteps outside her apartment door.
3. Things got worse and worse for Kim. Finally . . .

Skill Builder

J. In a word family, you find different forms of the same word. In the following example from the dictionary, what does the abbreviation *n.* mean? What does *v.* mean? What are two ways you can use the word *bat*?

> **bat** n. a strong stick used for hitting a ball
> v. to hit, as with a bat

Read the following dictionary entries. What do the abbreviations mean? Do you know the different meanings? Write a sentence using one of the forms of the word.

1. **clear** adj. 1. easy to see or understand. 2. not cloudy or dark.
   v. 1. to become clear. 2. to free.
   Example: _It's a clear day. There are no Clouds._

2. **shadow** n. 1. a dark image made when an object stops light.
   2. a person who follows someone.
   v. 1. to make dark or gloomy. 2. to follow someone.

   _____

   _____

3. **worry** v. 1. to bother. 2. to cause someone to feel anxious.
n. something that troubles someone.

_____

_____

4. **story** n. 1. the telling of something that happened; it can be
fiction or nonfiction. 2. all the rooms on the same level of
a building.

_____

_____

5. **repair** v. to fix or make better.
n. something that has been fixed.

_____

_____

More Reading

K. Now read the conclusion of "The Shadow." Take turns reading parts, like a play. The parts are as follows: a narrator, Kim, and Daniel.

THE SHADOW (continued)

Kim was scared. She was afraid to go outside now and afraid to be alone at night. One afternoon, she was thinking about calling the police when the phone rang.

A man's voice said, "Is this Kim Kang?"

"Yes, it is."

"Kim, this is Daniel Kang. I'd like to talk to you. I think you are my sister."

"What?" asked Kim. "Really? I do have a brother, but I've never seen him. I came to the U.S. before he was born. How do you know I'm your sister?"

The man said, "I saw you on a bus. I was on the sidewalk, and you looked out the window at me as the bus went by. I thought I had seen a ghost! You looked exactly like my mother. I jumped into a taxi and followed the bus so I could see where you lived and find out your name. I've come over to your apartment to see you many times, but I wasn't really sure who you were so I never tried to talk to you. Finally I decided to call you. Can we meet somewhere and talk?"

"You're the shadow!" said Kim.

"What?" said the voice.

"The shadow! The person who has been watching me. You made me so afraid! How can you prove you are my brother?"

"I have a picture of my mother," said the man. "Can we meet and I'll show it to you?"

Kim thought for a minute and then said, "OK, you can come to my office at noon tomorrow. It's the tall building on the corner of Park and Regent. I'll meet you outside, and we can talk. I hope you are my brother and my shadow, and that no one watches me anymore!"

Answer the following questions about the story.

1. What was Kim afraid to do?
2. Who was "the shadow"?
3. Kim doesn't know if Daniel is her brother. Why?
4. When did Daniel first see Kim?
5. Daniel thinks Kim is his sister. Why?
6. Why did Daniel jump into a taxi and follow Kim?
7. Why did Daniel go to Kim's apartment many times?
8. Do you believe Daniel? Why or why not?
9. Do you think Kim will go to the meeting? Would you go if you were Kim?

Extras

L. Use the following resources to explore more mysteries and riddles.

1. Alexander, L. G. *K's First Case*. Longman, Inc., 1982.
2. Draper, C. G., ed. *Great American Short Stories I: An ESL/EFL Reader*. Prentice-Hall, 1985. This reader includes Poe's "A Tell-Tale Heart," Harte's "Miggles," Stockton's "The Lady, or the Tiger?" and Bierce's "An Occurrence at Owl Creek Bridge."
3. Most film libraries have selections from Poe, Stockton, and Bierce.
4. Swann, Brian. *A Basket Full of White Eggs: Riddle-Poems*. Orchard Books, 1988.
5. Students can watch and discuss a television mystery, too—for example, "Murder, She Wrote."

2

Stories to Remember

Prereading

A. What do you think?

1. Discuss the meaning of the word *folktale*.

2. Do you know any folktales from your country or the U.S.? (For example: *Cinderella, Rip Van Winkle, Little Red Riding Hood*)
3. When and where do people first learn folktales?
4. Why do people tell folktales?
5. Look at the preceding picture and find the rice, corn, bamboo, and weeds. (These plants are important in the folktale, *Rice and Corn*, which follows.)

B. What does it mean? Before reading the folktale, look at the following sentences and guess the meanings of the underlined words. After reading *Rice and Corn*, write the meanings of the underlined words in the blanks *in your own words*.

1. "Please let us live!" they <u>begged</u> the farmer.

_____

_____

2. When the rice and corn plants were <u>as big as the feathers in a rooster's tail</u>, the bamboo, weeds, and trees began to grow again.

_____

_____

3. You planted us <u>in the heart of the forest</u>. We cannot grow here because it is too <u>crowded</u>.

_____

_____

4. Tell the bamboo, weeds, and trees not to <u>bother</u> or hurt you anymore because I am coming.

_____

_____

5. You can go home and <u>live in peace</u>.

_____

_____

6. Make a place for us to stay near your house. When we are <u>ripe</u>, we will come to you.

_____

_____

Reading

This folktale from the Hmong people of Laos has a *moral*, or a lesson to teach. Explain the moral when you have finished reading.

RICE AND CORN
As Told by Long Lee and Pheng Her

One day long ago, when all plants and animals could talk to each other, a Hmong farmer went out to get his field ready for planting. He began by cutting down the wild plants—the bamboo, the trees, and the weeds. The wild plants cried, "Please let us live!" They begged the farmer to stop, but he just kept cutting them down. When he had finished, he put them all together and burned them.

Then this farmer, who was just a little lazy, planted rice and corn in the field. Soon the rice and corn began to grow. But oh! When the little plants were as big as the feathers in a rooster's tail, all the wild plants began to grow again, too! Soon the weeds broke the little rice plants and took the sun and water away from the corn plants.

The rice and corn decided to go tell the farmer. "Mr.

Hmong farmer," said the rice and corn, "you planted us in the heart of the forest, but now the big old bamboo, the trees, and the weeds are growing there again. They are hitting us and breaking our hands and our feet. Why did you plant us there? If you don't help us, we won't be able to live."

"Oh, my dear corn and rice," said the farmer, "go back and wait for me. I will come and help you soon. Go and tell the bamboo, weeds, and trees not to bother or hurt you anymore because I am coming."

So the rice and corn went back to the forest field to talk to the wild plants. "Our owner is coming to see you," said the rice and corn. "If you don't stop hitting us, he will make big trouble for you."

Many days passed. The rice and corn waited and waited for the farmer. At last, the farmer came to the field. He cut the bamboo, weeds, and trees that bothered the rice and corn. The weeds cried, but the farmer just kept cutting.

After that, the rice and corn were happy. "Ah, Mr. Farmer," they said, "you have brought us back to life. Now you can go home and live in peace. There is only one thing left to do. Make a place for us to stay near your house. When we are ripe, we will come to you there. You won't have to come to the field to get us."

The farmer went home, and because he was tired and lazy, he went to bed. He lay in bed a long time—so long that his ears became flat. When the corn and rice were ripe, they came to him like a river of water, but there was no place for them to stay. They had to wait outside in the rain and get wet.

The rice and corn went to talk to the farmer. "There is no place for us to stay!" they said. "You didn't do what we asked you to do, so now we will go back to the field. Whenever you need something to eat, you will just have to come and get us."

The Hmong people say that this is why farmers have to carry the rice and corn from the faraway fields to their homes when they are hungry.

Exercises

Comprehension

C. The following sentences are about the story. They are not in the correct order. Work in groups and decide which sentence happened first, second, third, and so on. Write the correct number in the blank before each sentence.

____ The farmer didn't make a place near his house for the rice and corn.

____ The farmer finally came and cut down the bamboo, weeds, and trees that were bothering the rice and corn.

____ The corn and rice went to the farmer's house when they were ripe, but there was no place to stay.

_1_ The farmer went out to cut weeds and plant rice and corn.

____ The rice and corn went to talk to the farmer because the bamboo, weeds, and trees were growing again and bothering them.

____ The rice and corn said, "Now whenever you are hungry, you will have to go to the field and get us."

____ The rice and corn said to the farmer, "You have helped us. Now please make a place for us to live near your house."

D. In groups, discuss the following. Then share your answers with the class.

1. Describe the farmer in the story.
2. Why do Hmong farmers have to go to the field for rice and corn when they need food?
3. Does this story try to teach a lesson? If so, what is the lesson?

Vocabulary

E. Circle the letter of the sentence that means the same as the underlined word.

1. The farmer cut down the <u>weeds</u>.
   (a) rice and corn
   (b) plants he didn't want
   (c) tall trees

2. The weeds really <u>bothered</u> the rice and corn.
   (a) gave the rice and corn a lot of trouble
   (b) talked to the rice and corn
   (c) loved the rice and corn

3. When the corn and rice are <u>ripe</u>, we pick them.
   (a) growing
   (b) planting
   (c) fully grown

4. The corn and rice were in the <u>heart</u> of the forest.
   (a) end
   (b) center
   (c) beginning

5. I am the <u>owner</u> of this field.
   (a) I bought this field, and it is mine.
   (b) I want to buy this field.
   (c) I sold this field.

Listening

F. Books closed. Listen to the following folktale. You will hear it twice. Then you will be asked some questions about the story.

THE BEAUTIFUL MOUSE
A Hmong Folktale
As Told by Lue Thao

A long time ago, there was a family of mice—a mother, a father, and their daughter. This daughter was the most beautiful mouse in all the world. Her parents knew this, and they told her, "Because you are so beautiful, you must marry the most powerful one in all the world."

As the mouse grew up, she thought and thought about her parents' words. Finally, when she was old enough to marry, she went to the sun and said, "Oh, sun, you are the most powerful one in all the world. You must marry me."

"Oh, not I!" answered the sun. "The cloud is more powerful than I am. When I want to look at the earth, the cloud can stand in front of me, and I can't shine on the earth."

So the mouse went to the cloud. "Oh, cloud," she said. "You are the most powerful one in all the world. You must marry me."

"Oh, not I!" answered the cloud. "The wind is more powerful than I am. When I want to stay in one place, the wind comes and moves me."

So the mouse went to the wind, "Oh, wind," she said, "you are the most powerful one in all the world. You must marry me."

"Oh, not I!" said the wind. "The anthill is more powerful than I am. I cannot blow an anthill down."

So the mouse went to the anthill and said, "Oh, anthill, you are the most powerful one in all the world. You must marry me."

"Oh, not I!" answered the anthill. "The most powerful one in all the world is the mouse. The mouse is the only animal who can build its house in me."

So the beautiful mouse went back home and married a mouse. And they lived happily ever after.

Write the answers to the following questions as your teacher reads them aloud.

1. Why did the mouse's parents want her to marry the most powerful one in all the world?
2. Why did the sun say the cloud was more powerful?

3. Why did the cloud say the wind was more powerful?

4. Why did the wind say the anthill was more powerful?

5. Why was the mouse happy in the end?

Now open your books, read the story, and check your answers. With your classmates, decide if there is a lesson in this story.

Conversation

G. Prepare to tell a folktale to someone in your class. Make notes about the folktale. The following questions will help you write your notes.

1. What's the name of the story?
2. Where does the story happen? When?
3. Who are the characters in the story?
4. What happens
   (a) in the beginning of the story?
   (b) in the middle?
   (c) in the end?

Now use your notes to tell your story to a partner. Your partner can help you tell a good story by answering the following questions about it.

1. What do you think of your partner's story? Do you understand the story?
2. When and where does the story happen?
3. Do you feel that you know the characters in the story?
4. What are the characters like? Are they good, bad, or funny?
5. Is there a lesson in the story?
6. Did your partner leave anything out of the story?

Skill Builder

H. Quotation marks ("...") show exactly what someone says. Look at the following example and discuss the punctuation marks.

"Oh, sun. You are the most powerful one in all the world," said the mouse.

Read the following sentences and decide where to use quotation marks.

1. You planted us in the heart of the forest, said the rice and corn.
2. Oh, my dear corn and rice, said the farmer, go back and wait for me.
3. The rice and corn said to the wild plants, Stop hitting us or our owner will make trouble for you.
4. Ah, Mr. Farmer, said the rice and corn, you have brought us back to life.
5. The rice and corn talked to the farmer and said, We have come to you, and you have no place for us to stay!

Writing

I. Use your notes from exercise G to write a folktale. Try to use quotation marks in the story.

More Reading

J. Before you read this folktale, discuss the meanings of the following words and phrases.

useless	puzzle	whirlpool
to hide/hid	to solve	to feel ashamed
cave	trunk of a tree	lies

THE OLD PEOPLE
A Cambodian Folktale
As Told by Sinnary Veng

There once was a king who thought that old people were useless and no good. He decided to send all the old people in his country far, far away so that no one would ever see them again.

A very smart boy who worked in the king's house heard about the king's plan. The boy decided to hide his

father in a cave so the king couldn't find him and send him away.

Then one day, a king from another country came to visit. This king said, "I have a very difficult puzzle. We will both try to solve it. Whoever solves it will win and will be the best king in all the world." The first king loved puzzles and he loved to win, so he agreed to try the puzzle.

The king from another country brought out a piece of wood cut from the trunk of a tree and said, "Here is the puzzle. Which is the bottom of the piece of wood, and which is the top? You have two weeks to find the answer."

The first king tried and tried to solve the puzzle, but he couldn't. One day, the boy went to the cave to visit his father and told him about the puzzle. "Don't worry, my son. It is very easy," said the father. "Take the piece of wood and put it in a whirlpool in a river. The end that goes down first is the bottom because it is heavier."

The boy was very excited and ran back to the king and told him the answer to the puzzle. The king looked at the boy and said, "How did you know the answer? You are very young and don't know many things."

The boy, who never told lies, said, "My father told me, sir. He is very old, but he knows many things, and I love him very much. I hid him in a cave so you wouldn't send him away."

The king felt very ashamed, and he decided to stop sending the old people away. From that time on, old people have been the most important people in the country.

Answer the following questions about the story.

1. Why did the king send away all the old people?
2. How did the boy know about the king's plan?
3. Why did the king want to solve the puzzle?
4. What was the puzzle?
5. What was the answer to the puzzle?
6. What was the king's mistake? How did he feel?
7. What do you think is the lesson in this story?

Extras

K. Use the following books or videos to learn more about folktales.

1. Bierhorst, John. *The Naked Bear: Folktales of the Iroquois*. William Morrow, 1987.
2. Haley, Gail E. *A Story, A Story*. Collier Macmillan Canada, Inc., 1980.
3. Haviland, Virginia. *Favorite Fairy Tales Told Around the World*. Little, Brown & Co., 1985.
4. Vuong, Lynette Dyer. *The Brocaded Slipper and Other Vietnamese Tales*. Addison-Wesley, 1982.

Why the Sun Rises in the East and Sets in the West

Prereading

A. What do you think?

1. A *myth* is a story that explains something about *nature*, such as how the stars got into the sky or why the leaves change color in the autumn.

2. Read the title of the following story and tell what this myth will be about.

3. Why do you think the sun rises in the *east* and sets in the *west*?

B. What does it mean?

1. Identify the *owl, buffalo,* and *raven* in the preceding picture. Find the *Upper World* and the *Lower World*.

2. Read the following short paragraph and then discuss what the underlined words mean. Work with a classmate to draw this forest scene.

(1)<u>Darkness</u> is beginning in the forest. It is (2)<u>evening</u> and the sun is (3)<u>setting</u>. I am walking quietly; suddenly I see an owl hiding in the (4)<u>thick</u> branches of the tree. The owl thinks I can't see it. I make a noise, but the owl (5)<u>refuses</u> to move.

Reading

WHY THE SUN RISES IN THE EAST AND SETS IN THE WEST

Long, long ago, there were two worlds, the Upper World and the Lower World. The sun lived in the Upper World. All the plants and animals lived in the Lower World, where it was cold and dark. Only a little of the sun's light was able to get through the clouds between the two worlds.

The animals were always complaining because they were cold and hungry. One day, the owl told the other animals about a time when life was different in the Lower World.

"My grandfather told me about a time long ago when the Lower World had a sun as bright as fire. It filled the Lower World with light and warmth," said the owl.

"Where is this sun now?" asked the buffalo.

The owl, who was very wise, said, "It is hiding from us in the Upper World. It refuses to shine on this World."

"Then we must go talk to the sun," said the buffalo. "We will ask the sun to shine on us again."

The animals then argued about which of them would go to find the sun. No one wanted to go. Finally they decided the raven should go because he had strong, black wings and was very intelligent.

So the raven flew to where the Upper World began and pushed a hole through the thick, black clouds. He flew through the hole and saw the sun shining so brightly that he had to cover his eyes with his wings.

"Sun, I have come to ask you to shine upon us in the Lower World," said the raven. "We are cold all the time. It is always dark. The plants have trouble growing, and the animals are weak and hungry."

"Long ago I went to the Lower World where you live," answered the sun. "I stayed there for many years, but I didn't like it. I traveled from north to south and back again. In the northern part of the Lower World, my light was very weak, and it was always cold. In the southern part, my light was very strong, and there was too much heat. So I decided to live here in the Upper World, where it is not too hot and not too cold."

"I have an idea!" said the raven. "You will like the Lower World if you travel from east to west, not from north to south as you did before. Come. Follow me. I will show you."

So the clouds opened, and the sun followed the raven to the Lower World. They traveled across the Lower World for twenty-four hours, always moving from east to west. Sunshine filled the Lower World for part of the day; then darkness returned at night. It was not too hot and not too cold. The sun enjoyed his daily trip, and soon the Lower World was filled with green plants and many kinds of animals. From that time until now, the sun has risen each day in the east and set each evening in the west.

Exercises

Comprehension

C. Write *T* for true and *F* for false.

_____ 1. The sun was hiding in the Lower World.
_____ 2. All the animals remembered a time when the sun was as bright as fire in their World.
_____ 3. All the animals wanted to go find the sun.
_____ 4. The animals wanted the raven to go because he was strong and intelligent.
_____ 5. The raven had trouble finding the sun because the sun's light was very weak.
_____ 6. When the sun traveled from east to west, it was not too hot and not too cold in the Lower World.

D. Discuss the following.

1. Describe the Lower World.
2. What problem did the animals have?
3. What did they decide to do about their problem?
4. Why did they make that decision?
5. Where did the raven find the sun?
6. What did the raven say to the sun?

Vocabulary

E. Find the *opposite* of each word listed and write the correct letter in each blank.

_____ 1. to argue   a. to lower
_____ 2. strong   b. to say that everything is going well
_____ 3. intelligent   c. to set
_____ 4. to complain   d. weak

---- 5. upper   e. thin
---- 6. thick   f. stupid
---- 7. to rise   g. to agree

Listening

F. Books open. You will hear the following paragraphs from "Why the Sun Rises in the East and Sets in the West" two times. The first time, listen. The second time, write the missing words in the blanks. Then turn to paragraph seven in the story to check your work.

The animals then (1) _____ about which one of them (2) _____ go to find the sun. (3) _____ wanted to go. Finally they (4) _____ the raven should go because he had (5) _____, black wings and was very (6) _____.

So the raven flew to where the Upper (7) _____ began and pushed a hole through the (8) _____, black clouds. He flew through the (9) _____ and saw the sun shining so (10) _____ that he had to cover his eyes with his (11) _____.

Conversation

G. In American culture, some animals have certain personalities. For example, the owl is wise, and the mule is stubborn. Work in groups of three or four to complete the following chart about animal personalities in different cultures. Add the names of some other animals, if you wish. When you are finished, compare charts.

	United States	Culture 1	Culture 2
ox	*strong*	_____	_____
goose	*silly*	_____	_____
dog	*true friend*	_____	_____
	faithful		
cat	*lazy*	_____	_____
pig	*dirty*	_____	_____
fox	*sly*	_____	_____
lion	*brave*	_____	_____
_____	_____	_____	_____
_____	_____	_____	_____
_____	_____	_____	_____

Writing

H. Think about a story from your culture that explains something in nature or describe a myth you have read. Work with a partner and tell each other your stories. Choose one to write about. Make a list of what happens at the beginning, the middle, and the end of the story. Next, write the story together. When you are finished, test your story with the following questions:

1. Is the story interesting or funny?
2. Do the people or animals in the story seem real or believable?
3. Does the story explain something in nature?

Skill Builder

I. Answer the following questions about this textbook.

1. What information do you find on the title page of this book?
2. What is the date of publication?
3. Where was the book published?
4. Look at the table of contents. What three different kinds of readings are there in this book?
5. If you want to improve your newspaper reading skills, what chapters should you read?
6. If you want to read poetry, what chapter should you read?
7. What kind of information do you find in the introduction of this book?
8. How do the pictures in this book help you understand the readings?

More Reading

J. Discuss what it means to *lose patience* and *to be reminded of*. Then read the following myth about the god of love.

WHERE THE CLOUDS CAME FROM

The god of love was losing patience with the people of the world. He told them again and again that they must learn to love each other. They must learn to work together and take care of their world.

The people seemed to listen to the god of love, and they did try to get along for awhile. But soon they forgot his words and began to fight again. Brothers and sisters fought, cities fought, and countries fought. The people were hurting each other and their beautiful world.

One day, as the god of love watched the beginning of another war in the world, he lost his patience. He decided to stop talking to the people and do something which would always remind them of his words.

He flew down on the world and carried the people who were fighting up into the sky. He turned them into big, soft, fluffy clouds in many different shapes. Now they could hit each other without hurting the beautiful world. Their thunder and lightning would remind people of the terrible power of war, but their snow and rain would feed, rather than hurt, the world.

Discuss the following questions.

1. What did the god of love tell the people of the world?
2. What did the people of the world always do?
3. What did the god of love do when he lost his patience?
4. What will the thunder and lightning remind people of?
5. What will the clouds give to the world?

Extras

K. Use the following books to learn more about myths.

1. Abayom, Fuja. *Fourteen Hundred Cowries and Other African Tales.* Lothrop, Lee & Shepard Co., 1971.
2. Bierhorst, John. *The Hungry Woman, Myths and Legends of the Aztecs.* William Morrow & Co., 1984.
3. Hamilton, Virginia. *In the Beginning.* Harcourt Brace Jovanovich, 1988.
4. Hodges, Margaret. *The Other World, Myths of the Celts.* Farrar, Straus & Giroux, 1973.
5. McDermott, Gerald. *Arrow to the Sun, a Pueblo Indian Tale.* Viking Penguin Inc., 1974.
6. Monroe, Jean Guard. *They Dance in the Sky.* Houghton Mifflin, 1987.

4

Introduction to Poetry

A. What do you think?

1. This chapter is about poetry. Look at the readings quickly and then answer the question, "What is a poem?"
2. The poems in this chapter have both *rhyme* and *rhythm*. In the first poem, look at the last word in each line. Which words rhyme?

3. Now find the rhyme pattern in the first poem. Is there a rhyming word at the end of every line, or is it every other line?

4. What is the rhythm of the first poem? (How many syllables are there in each line?)

5. Sometimes words are used in new ways in a poem. For example, a poet might say the sky was "pregnant with rain" or that "the moon sailed across a sea of clouds." Watch for this in the poems that follow.

6. When you read a poem, sometimes you get a special feeling from it. Make a list of all the words you can think of that describe feelings (for example: lonely, joyful, and so forth). After reading each poem in this chapter, decide how the poem makes you feel.

B. What does it mean? Before reading the first poem, discuss the meanings of the following words.

to lean	lonely
cruel	wool
to blow away	

Reading

After you read this poem, be ready to explain how the poet paints a picture for the reader.

Birch Trees*

John Richard Moreland

The night is white,
The moon is high.
The birch trees lean
Against the sky.

The cruel winds
Have blown away

---

* From *The Home Book of Verse for Young Folks* by Burton Egbert Stevenson. Copyright 1957 by Holt, Rinehart and Winston.

Each little leaf
Of silver gray.

O lonely trees
As white as wool . . .
That moonlight makes
So beautiful.

Exercises

Comprehension

C. Answer the following questions about "Birch Trees."

1. What season is it?
2. Why is the wind cruel?
3. Find words used in new ways in the poem.
   Example: *night is white*
   birch trees lean against the sky.

   _____

   _____

4. How do the birch trees make the poet feel?
5. How does "Birch Trees" make you feel? (Use words from exercise A, item 6.)

D. What does it mean? Before reading the next poem, discuss the meanings of the following words.

to fling your arms wide	slim
to whirl	gently
pale	tenderly

Reading

The following poem was written by Langston Hughes, a well-known black American poet. Remember the title as you read the poem.

Dream Variation*

Langston Hughes

To fling my arms wide
In some place of the sun,
To whirl and to dance
Till the white day is done.

Then rest at cool evening
Beneath a tall tree
While night comes on gently,
*   Dark like me—*
That is my dream!

To fling my arms wide
In the face of the sun,
Dance! whirl! whirl!
Till the quick day is done.
Rest at pale evening . . .
A tall, slim tree,
Night coming tenderly
*   Black like me.*

Exercises

Comprehension

E. Answer the following questions about *Dream Variation*.

1. In the poem, the day is the time for _____, and the early evening is the time for _____.

2. Find words used in new ways in the poem.
   Example: *quick day*
   _____
   _____
   _____

3. This poem has many opposites, such as white day/dark night. Make a list of other opposites in the poem.

4. How does the poem make you feel?

5. Why is the poem called *Dream Variation*?

Vocabulary

F. Find the word or phrase that means the same as each word listed and write the correct letter in each blank.

___ 1. slim	a.	not kind, mean
___ 2. cruel	b.	without friends, alone
___ 3. pale	c.	to sit or stand with your weight against something
___ 4. to whirl		
___ 5. lonely	d.	thin
___ 6. gently	e.	to go round and round in a circle
___ 7. to lean against		
	f.	softly, not roughly
	g.	without color

Listening

G. Books open. Work in pairs—one person is *A*, and one is *B*. Follow the directions to practice reading and writing the poems.

1. *A* slowly reads the first part of *Birch Trees* while *B* writes the poem.
2. Check *B's* work together.
3. *B* reads the first part of *Dream Variations* while *A* writes the poem.
4. Check *A's* work together.

Conversation

H. Sayings and *proverbs* (a saying with a lesson) use words and sounds in unusual ways, just as poems do. What is the meaning of this saying?

All's well that ends well.

What is the lesson in this proverb?

An apple a day keeps the doctor away.

What do you notice about the rhymes or repeated sounds in the preceding sayings? In small groups, discuss the meanings of the following sayings and proverbs.

1. Like father, like son.
2. Easier said than done.
3. A place for everything and everything in its place.
4. Practice makes perfect.
5. A penny saved is a penny earned.

Think of other sayings and proverbs and then share them with the class. You may want to translate some from your first language.

Writing

I. Poems come in many forms and from many cultures.

1. Haiku is a kind of poetry from Japan. Haiku is usually about the natural world (weather, seasons, and so forth), and each poem has 17 syllables. Read this example of Haiku and answer the questions that follow.

> *Gentle morning rain*
> *Black-tipped, snow-white stork flying*
> *Into the rainbow.*

    (a) What things from nature do you "see" when you read this poem?
    (b) How many syllables does it have
        in the first line?
        in the second line?
        in the third line?
        in all?

2. Complete the following Haiku-style poem about evening. Then share your poems by reading them aloud.

> *Huge red sun falling,*
> *Filling all the evening sky*

_____

(Write five more syllables about the sun or sky. You might explain how or where the sun falls.)

3. Write your own Haiku-style poem about a season or a time of day. Write so that the reader will "see" a picture from the natural world. Write three lines, but do not worry about how many syllables you put in each line. You can write about a place or an experience you remember.

_____

_____

_____

J. Sometimes people use words to make a picture-poem. Read the following poem about Chicago. Why are the words written *where* they are? Write a picture-poem about a city you know.

Skill Builder

K. Go to a library to see what kinds of poetry books are there. Follow these directions.

1. Look up *poetry* in the card catalog.
2. Notice the call numbers in the upper left-hand corner of the cards under *poetry*.
3. Using the call numbers, find the poetry section of the library.
4. Write down the title and author's name of one poetry book that looks interesting. Later, explain to the class why the book looked interesting.

More Reading

L. Read the following poems aloud, in groups or as a class, and answer the questions.

Thirty days hath September,
April, June, and November.
All the rest have thirty-one
Except February, which has twenty-eight.

1. How many months have 30 days? 31 days?
2. Why is this poem useful?

*There was a young lady from Riga**
Who rode with a smile on a tiger;
    They returned from the ride
    With the lady inside
And the smile on the face of the tiger.

Anonymous (before 1888)

1. What is Riga?
2. What did the lady do for fun one day?

---

* From *The Book of Nonsense* by Roger Lancelyn Green. Copyright © 1956 by J.M. Dent & Sons Ltd., renewed 1984 by Roger Lancelyn Green. Reprinted by permission of the publishers, Dutton Children's Books, a division of Penguin Books USA Inc. and J.M. Dent & Sons Ltd., England.

3. Why was she smiling?
4. What happened during the ride?
5. Why was the tiger smiling?

Extras

M. Selections from the following books can be read aloud in class.

1. Adoff, Arnold. *All the Colors of the Race*. Lothrop, Lee & Shepard, 1982.
2. Bierhorst, John, ed. *The Sacred Path: Spells, Prayers and Power Songs of the American Indians*. William Morrow & Co., 1983.
3. Pomerantz, Charlotte. *If I had a Paka: Poems in Eleven Languages*. Greenwillow, 1982.
4. Silverstein, Shel. *Where the Sidewalk Ends*. Harper & Row, 1974.
5. Viorst, Judith. *If I Were In Charge of the World*. Atheneum Publishers, 1983.

5

A Special Person

Prereading

A. What do you think?

1. Sometimes babies are born with a problem called Down's syndrome. These children are different—they learn slowly, and they may have problems with some part of their body. Do you

know a person with Down's syndrome? Use this information to discuss Down's syndrome.

2. The families of children with Down's syndrome have special worries and problems. For example, the Down's syndrome child will never be able to live alone as an adult. What are some other problems for the families of Down's syndrome children?

B. What does it mean? Divide into groups of three and guess the meanings of the following words. You may need to find some of the words in the story "A Special Person," which follows. Teach the words you know to students in another group.

diagnosis
to recommend
to agree
instead
cheerfully

Reading

A SPECIAL PERSON

When parents learn that their new baby has Down's syndrome, their whole world changes.

It was that way when Monte was born. Five days after Monte's birth, the doctor explained the diagnosis to his parents. The doctor recommended sending Monte away, to a special home. Monte would live there always—without his parents.

Some of Monte's relatives agreed with the doctor. They thought Monte's parents should send him to a special home right away. They thought it would be too hard to take care of him at home. Monte's parents listened to a nurse instead. She told them what Monte needed most—to stay with his own loving family.

She was so right.

Monte was easy to love right from the beginning. He

was a gentle boy who didn't like to fight. Once when some little girls threw sand at him in the park, Monte just quietly picked up his things and walked home.

Monte did the usual things all children do; he just did them later. However, Monte learned one thing very early—he started school at three and learned to read at four! Today, Monte reads very well. He loves to go to the library and often reads books about the Civil War and World War II. He also reads the newspaper and the Bible every day. Math is harder for Monte, but he can do both addition and subtraction.

Monte spends his days like most people his age (27); the only difference is he can't work now because of a heart condition. He does the laundry, cleans a little, and cooks sometimes. If you call his house, he's usually the one to answer the phone. He always says cheerfully, "Hello, This is the Riggert's. Monte speaking."

Monte has brought a lot of happiness to his family. They know they made the right decision.

Exercises

Comprehension

C. Answer the following questions.

1. When did Monte's parents find out he had Down's syndrome?
2. What did the doctor and Monte's relatives recommend?
3. What did a nurse recommend?
4. Why was Monte easy to love?
5. How was Monte the same as other children?
6. What is Monte interested in?
7. How old is Monte today? What is his life like?
8. What decision did Monte's parents make? Why do they think they made the right decision?

D. Discuss the following questions.

1. What different kinds of feelings do you think Monte's parents had when he was born?
2. Why do you think the doctor recommended a special home for Monte?
3. Why did Monte's parents take him home with them?
4. Why do you think Monte is so cheerful on the phone?
5. Do you think Monte's parents made the right decision? Why or why not?

Vocabulary

E. Read the following sentences about Monte. Then rewrite the sentence in your own words, or just explain the underlined words.
Example: Monte was <u>born</u> 27 years ago.

Monte was a new baby 27 years ago.

1. Monte was born with <u>Down's syndrome</u>.
2. The doctor <u>recommended</u> that Monte live in a special home away from his family.
3. Many of Monte's <u>relatives</u> agreed with the doctor.
4. <u>Instead of</u> taking Monte to a <u>special home</u>, his parents took him home with them.
5. Monte reads the newspaper and the <u>Bible</u> every day.
6. Monte can't work now because he has a heart <u>condition</u>.

Listening

F. Books closed. Listen to two short stories about Monte. After each story, you will be asked three questions about it.

1. Monte could not learn to ride a bike, so his parents bought a bicycle-for-two from a neighbor. Once, Monte and his dad, David, were on the bike together, and they rode into some sand along a bike path. When they tried to turn, they both fell down in the sand. Monte's dad began to laugh, but Monte said in his most adult voice, "David, that wasn't one bit funny."

Now write the answers to the following questions.
  (a) What kind of bike was Monte riding?
  (b) Why did Monte and his dad fall off the bike?
  (c) Did Monte think falling down was funny?

Discuss the words *wheelchair* and *pride* before listening to this story.

2. Because Monte has a heart condition, he sometimes has trouble walking very far. So a neighbor gave him a wheelchair to use. One day when Monte was staying with his sister, his niece and his nephew wanted to push him around outside in the wheelchair. Monte said, "No! Wait until your mother comes out to help." But because the children were young, they didn't listen. They pushed him out of the garage and down the driveway so fast that Monte fell out of the chair. His sister came running out of the house shouting, "Monte! Are your hurt?" Monte quietly said, "No, just my pride."

Now write the answers to the following questions.
  (a) Why did Monte have to use a wheelchair sometimes?
  (b) How did Monte fall out of the wheelchair?
  (c) What part of Monte was hurt?

Conversation

G. In your country, what kind of a life do people like Monte have? Discuss the following chart, fill in the blanks for your country, and then compare information.

	U.S.	Your country
1. Medical care	Family doctor	_____
2. Place to live	At home	_____
	Group home	_____
	Full-care center	_____
3. Schooling	Public schools	_____
	Special schools	_____
4. Employment	Many small	_____
	businesses	_____
	(restaurants,	_____
	hospitals)	_____
5. Attitude	Most people are	_____
	kind.	_____
	Children can be	_____
	mean.	_____
	Many people stare.	_____

Writing

H. Later in this chapter, you will read a story about Monte getting lost. Did you or anyone in your family ever get lost? In pairs, talk about your experience, or imagine getting lost. Describe what happened at the beginning, middle, and end of your experience. Then write a short paragraph about getting lost. Begin your paragraph as shown here. (You can change *I* to *my sister* or *my son*, and so forth.)

Once when I was _____, I got lost.

_____

_____

_____

_____

_____

_____

Skill Builder

I. Monte doesn't understand money very well, but he loves to go to the store. Work in groups to help him decide how much money he has, what he can buy, and how much change he will get.

1. He has four $1 bills and four quarters.
   How much does he have? _____
   What can he buy?
   (a) a book for $3.75, tax included
   (b) candy and soda for $5.05
   (c) two frozen pizzas for $6.34

   How much change will he get? _____

2. He has a $20 bill, six $1 bills, and two dimes.
   How much does he have? _____
   What can he buy?
   (a) a shirt on sale for $26.99, without tax
   (b) a pair of running shoes for $38.75, tax included
   (c) a pair of jeans for $25.99, tax included

   How much change will he get? _____

3. Monte has a $10 bill and five pennies.
   How much does he have? _____
   What can he buy?
   (a) toothpaste, soap, and shaving cream for $14.99, tax included
   (b) cards, paper, pencils, and pens for $5.33, tax included
   (c) film, magazines, a newspaper, and batteries for $10.10, tax included

   How much change will he get? _____

4. He has two $20 bills, a $5 bill, two $1 bills, a quarter, and two dimes.

   How much does he have? _____

   What can he buy? _____

   (a) a computer program for $23.50 and a cassette tape for $12.50, tax included

   (b) two computer programs for $24.00 each, tax included

   (c) a radio for $48.85, tax included

   How much change will he get? _____

5. Now write a problem of your own and ask students in another group to answer the questions.

   Monte has _____

                   (What bills and coins?)

   How much does he have? _____

   What can he buy? _____

   (a) _____

   (b) _____

   (c) _____

   How much change will he get? _____

More Reading

J. Before reading about Monte again, guess what the title and the picture tell you about this story.

MONTE'S ADVENTURES

Monte never had any fear of getting lost. When he went out with his family, he might just walk away when no one was watching. When Monte was 10, his dad took him to the county fair. They went to look at the cattle in one of the barns. Monte's dad started talking with some friends and didn't notice Monte slip away. Monte was gone for two hours while his dad and the sheriff were looking for him everywhere. Monte had climbed into someone's truck and was fast asleep on the front seat. The truck owner found him and took him to the sheriff's office, where Monte met his worried dad.

When Monte was eight or nine, he loved going to the grocery store. He often tried to slip off and get his own cart to fill up—if he could work that fast before his family found him! Once, he walked alone to the store about three blocks from his house. He got a grocery cart and filled it up with all his favorite food, like cookies and pizza. He also remembered to get some beer for his dad! Then Monte checked out at the cashier but couldn't pay. He didn't have any money! Luckily, one of his parents' friends was in the store, and she saw what had happened. She explained everything and then brought Monte home.

Discuss the following.

1. Why is this story named "Monte's Adventures"?
2. Write three other questions to ask about the story. Ask your classmates these questions.
3. Read the story again. Work with a partner and explain one of Monte's adventures in your own words. You tell one adventure, and then listen to your partner tell the other. Listen carefully to make sure all the details are correct.

4. Complete the following crossword puzzle with vocabulary
   words from "Monte's Adventures." Words to choose from are
   at the top, and definitions are at the bottom.

fear	slip away	cart
county fair	notice	checked out
cattle	sheriff	cashier
barn	worried	

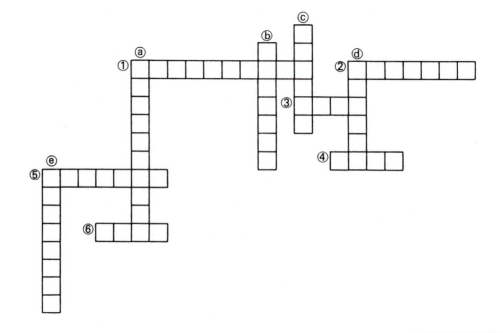

Across

1. went to the cash register and found out how much to pay
2. person who runs the cash register
3. something to carry groceries in
4. you have this feeling when you are afraid
5. someone like a police officer
6. a special building for animals

Down

a. an animal show and a festival
b. Monte's father felt this way when he was looking for Monte
c. see
d. cows
e. walk away quietly

Extras

K. Learn more about handicapped people by using the following resources.

1. Adams, Barbara. *Like It Is: Facts and Feelings About Handicaps from Kids Who Know.* Walker & Co., 1979.
2. *Bill* (1980), starring Mickey Rooney, is a moving film (or video) about an adult retarded person.
3. Kraus, Bob, ed. *An Exceptional View of Life: The Easter Seal Story.* Norfolk Island, Australia: Island Heritage Ltd., 1977.
4. Roy, Ron. *Move Over, Wheelchairs Coming Through!* Clarion, 1985.

6

Students in Taiwan

Michal Heron

Prereading

A. What do you think?

1. Find Taiwan on a map. What countries are nearby?
2. School *discipline* is different in different countries. What do you know about discipline in U.S. schools? What is discipline like in your country's schools?

3. Look at the picture and read the title of this chapter. Then write three questions that will probably be answered in the reading.
   Example: *How long is the school day in Taiwan?*

   _____

   _____

   _____

B. What does it mean? Quickly read the first two sentences in each paragraph of "Students in Taiwan." Find four to six words that you don't know but that are important to the meaning of the story. Work with other students to explain the meanings of those words.

Reading

STUDENTS IN TAIWAN

Most students in Taiwan study very hard both during and after school. High school students, for example, study at school from 7:30 A.M. to 4:00 P.M. Then, many attend private schools from about 5:30 P.M. to 7:30 P.M. When they return home, they still have homework to do. Sometimes they don't finish studying until very late at night.

Rose, Emily, and Kim are now students in American schools, but they all have been students in Taiwan. Recently, they talked about their school days in Taiwan. Rose said, "There are some important differences between Taiwanese and American schools. For example, the students stay in one classroom all day, and the teachers move from room to room. Students wear uniforms to school and have lots of cleaning to do at school every day. Also, some of the older teachers hit students on the open hand with a bamboo stick if the students are late or talk too much."

Emily explained that the teachers don't use a stick much anymore. "I only got hit twice in 10 years, but it was different for my brother. He was in trouble almost every day. He never did all his work, and he couldn't stop talking." Then Emily talked about another way of disciplining students in Taiwanese schools. She said, "Some days there is a special time when the students talk about other students in front of the class. Students take turns telling other students how to improve. One student complained about me, saying that I was bossy and violent. I didn't like that part of school."

Kim added, "Another important difference is that the students in Taiwan have many school duties. Our class had many student officials, such as president, vice-president, student disciplinarian, sanitary official, and assistant teacher. The whole class elects these officials. Usually the best students get these jobs each year.

"Let me explain what some of these officials do. There is a sanitary official because students must clean the school twice a day. They clean windows, tables, the floor, and the blackboard. And some weeks they must also clean the playground, the bathrooms, the garden, and the teachers' offices. The student disciplinarian helps keep the students quiet during self-study. The disciplinarian also checks to see that their hair, finger-nails, and uniforms are OK because students can't wear jewelry or have unusual hairstyles."

Rose finished the discussion by saying, "I think the biggest difference is the pressure. In Taiwan, students feel a lot of pressure from themselves, from their parents, and from their teachers—pressure to do well in school and to pass the exams. Only 40 percent of all high school students pass the exam for college. I know this sounds like very hard work, but we enjoyed our school years in Taiwan. I think those schools helped us to become responsible people."

Exercises

Comprehension

C. Discuss the following questions.

1. Why is it hard to be a student in Taiwan?

2. Name three ways that schools in Taiwan are different from American schools.
3. How do teachers discipline students in Taiwanese schools?
4. How do Taiwanese students discipline each other?
5. Why do Taiwanese students study so much?

D. Look back at the questions you wrote for exercise A, item 3. Decide if the answers are in the story.

Vocabulary

E. Find the *opposite* of each word listed and write the correct letter in each blank. Then discuss the meanings of the words.

____ 1. private	a.	not careful or thoughtful
____ 2. take turns	b.	always let the same person go first
____ 3. improve		
____ 4. violent	c.	peaceful
____ 5. responsible	d.	get worse
____ 6. recently	e.	public
	f.	a long time ago

F. Read the following sentences. Discuss the meanings of the underlined words. Then try to make other sentences using those words.

1. Students feel a lot of <u>pressure</u> from themselves, from their teachers, and from their parents to do well in school and pass the exams.
2. One student <u>complained</u> about me, saying that I was <u>bossy</u> and too violent.
3. The whole class <u>elects</u> the <u>officials</u>.
4. Students in Taiwan have many school <u>duties</u>.
5. Then Emily talked about another way of <u>disciplining</u> students in Taiwanese schools.

Listening

G. Books closed. Listen to the following information about U.S. schools. You will hear it twice. Listen for facts.

In the U.S., children begin school at age five. In elementary school, they study math, reading, science, social studies, and many special subjects, like art and music. They usually don't begin to study a foreign language until the sixth or the seventh grade. Many students in American middle schools and high schools *do* study a foreign language. They usually choose Spanish or French. Some schools also teach German or Latin. Many Americans think students wait too long to begin studying another language. And they think that schools should also teach languages like Chinese and Japanese.

Now you will hear three unfinished sentences. Write down the letter of the best ending for each sentence.

1. U.S. Children begin school at age _____.
   (a) five
   (b) eight
   (c) three

2. American students usually begin to study a foreign language in _____.
   (a) first or second grade
   (b) sixth or seventh grade
   (c) eleventh or twelfth grade

3. Students in American middle schools and high schools usually can study _____.
   (a) Spanish or French
   (b) Chinese or Japanese
   (c) Italian and Greek

After you check your answers, discuss the following questions.

1. When do you think Americans should start studying a foreign language? Why?
2. What languages do you think Americans should study? Why?

Conversation

H. Discuss the following questions.

1. Do you think schools in Taiwan are good? Why or why not?
2. Would you like school uniforms for yourself or your children?
3. What kind of discipline would you like in U.S. schools?
4. Why do you think that students in Taiwan do the cleaning work? Should students in American schools help clean the schools? Explain your answer.
5. Rose said, "I think those schools helped us to become responsible people." Why does she think that?

I. What do you want to know about schools in each others' countries? As a class, make a list of questions to ask each other.
Example: *At what age do children begin school in your country?*
Do families pay for school?

Now use the questions to interview a classmate. Take notes so that you can remember the important information. Finally, complete the following chart with your information. Add columns for more countries if necessary.

	Country 1	Country 2	Country 3
Hours at school	_____	_____	_____
Uniforms	_____	_____	_____
How much homework?	_____	_____	_____
_____	_____	_____	_____
_____	_____	_____	_____

Writing

J. Write about schools in your country. Complete the following two paragraphs, and add another paragraph if you have more ideas.

　　　　Schools in _____ are different from American schools. For example, students attend school each day from _____ to _____. The subjects students have every day are _____, _____, and _____. After school, students _____. Students feel _____ pressure from their parents to do well in school, so students _____.

　　　　There are some other important differences between schools in _____ and schools in the United States. One difference is _____

_____

_____

Another difference is _____

_____

_____

Skill Builder

K. Make a chart of the native country, the nationality, and the first language of each student in your class. Practice the words.

Country	Nationality	First Language
Taiwan	Taiwanese	Chinese/Taiwanese
U.S.	American	English
_____	_____	_____
_____	_____	_____

WHO photo by Bob Miller

More Reading

L. Read the following paragraphs to learn more about high school in Taiwan. Be ready to talk about why you would or would not like to be a student in Taiwan. Talk about the following words before you read.

> flag raising ceremony
> events
> manual training
> to take a nap

THE HIGH SCHOOL DAY IN TAIWAN

Students arrive at school at about 7:30 A.M. First there is a flag raising ceremony and then students listen to the principal. The principal talks about why it is necessary to be a good student. The principal also discusses important events in both the school and the country. Then there is a study time for half an hour. After that, students have classes from about 8:30 A.M. to 12:00 noon. When the students are in the classroom, the room is usually quiet. The students listen and take notes while the teacher explains the day's lesson.

In a high school in Taiwan, students study many different subjects. For example, in the tenth grade, students take Chinese, English, math, science, history, music, art, writing, home economics, manual training, physical education, and army training.

Lunch lasts for half an hour. Then students take a nap for 30 minutes. During the nap, students must put their heads down on their desks and be quiet. After the nap, classes start at about 1:00 P.M. and end at about 4:30 P.M. Then students are free to go home—or on some days, they have to stay and clean the school.

In Taiwan, education is very important to everyone. A student's day is only half over after school. Students, with the help of their families, work hard until about midnight every day.

Discuss the following.

1. Talk about any words or phrases in the above passage you still don't understand.
2. What do you think students learn in manual training and army training?
3. Discuss the reasons why you would or would not like to be a student in Taiwan.

Extras

M. Use the following resources to learn more about Taiwan.

1. Yu, Ling. *Taiwan in Pictures.* Lerner Publications, 1989.
2. Schreider, Helen and Frank. *The Watchful Dragon* in *National Geographic*, 135 (January 1969), 1.

7

A Dozen Babies

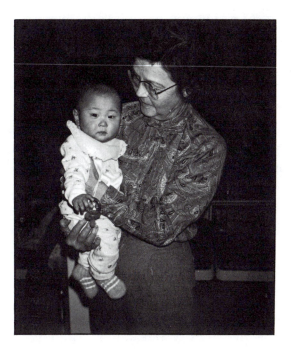

Prereading

A. What do you think?

1. What does it mean *to adopt* a baby? Do you know anyone who has adopted a baby?
2. Why do families adopt children? And why do families put their children up for adoption?

3. Is it easy to adopt a baby in your country? Why or why not?

4. The reading in this chapter is about babies adopted from Korea. Locate Seoul, Korea; Tokyo, Japan; and Chicago, Illinois on a map.

B. What does it mean? Read the following sentences and decide what the underlined words mean.

1. This baby is 11 months old. He'll have a birthday (a) <u>pretty soon</u>. Then he'll be one year old. The baby can't walk yet. He still (b) <u>crawls</u> to get around.

2. Thank you for (c) <u>offering</u> to take care of my baby for a few hours. I (d) <u>trust</u> you to take care of him. I know that you'll watch him carefully.

3. A new baby is a lot of work—feeding, (e) <u>changing</u>, comforting, and washing a baby is a full-time job.

4. A new baby makes parents very tired. There's so much to do that they feel they (f) <u>need extra hands</u>.

5. Can you (g) <u>imagine</u> having twin babies?

Reading

An American grandmother traveling from Seoul, Korea to Chicago, Illinois sent this letter to her daughter, Sally.

A DOZEN BABIES

Dear Sally,

Every day of our trip to Korea has been more interesting than the one before — including our flight home from Seoul to Chicago. Our first stop was the Tokyo airport, and we found twelve Korean babies in the waiting room! They were about six to nine months old and they were all moving at once. Some were crying; others were crawling. Three American adults were trying to take care of all the babies. They were changing diapers, feeding the babies and chasing the babies who were crawling. If one baby started to cry, all the others began to cry too. A lot of people were standing nearby watching the three Americans trying to take care of all the babies.

At first, I just watched too. Then I decided to ask if I could help. As soon as I asked, they put a big, strong baby into my arms. I was a little surprised that the adults trusted me, but they really needed some extra hands. Other people began to help too. A tall, young man offered to help and pretty soon he was holding a sweet, tiny baby. I asked him if we could trade babies because 'mine' was so big and I was so small! He was happy to give me the little one to hold.

The babies all had brown skin, black hair and bright, black eyes. They all wore cotton, flowered shirts and diapers. They were friendly, and very happy to have someone hold them and talk to them. Earlier that day, the babies had flown from Seoul to Tokyo, and they had thirteen more hours to fly before they reached Chicago. Each baby was already adopted by an American family.

I offered to help with the babies on the long flight to Chicago too, but I wasn't needed. When we landed in Chicago, the new families were waiting in the airport, but we didn't see any of the new parents. They were waiting for everyone to leave before they got on the plane to see their new baby for the first time. Can you imagine how they felt? I wonder how those babies will grow up in the U.S. I'm sure the experience will be very different for each one.

We'll talk more about my trip when I see you in three weeks.

Love,
Mom

Exercises

Comprehension

C. Write *T* for true and *F* for false.

____ 1. The babies were traveling from Korea to the U.S.
____ 2. The 12 babies were on vacation.
____ 3. The three adults had trouble taking care of a dozen babies.
____ 4. The babies were shy and unfriendly.
____ 5. One American family adopted a dozen babies.
____ 6. The new families were waiting at the airport in Tokyo.

D. Discuss the following questions.

1. The babies are from Korea. Why are they going to the U.S.?
2. Why did the American grandmother offer to help?
3. Why did the three adults trust the grandmother and give her a baby to hold?
4. Describe the babies.
5. How do you think the new parents felt while they were waiting in the airport for their new babies?

Vocabulary

E. Work in groups of four or five. In the following list, there is a synonym (a word or words that mean the same) for each word or phrase. Write each item on the list on a three-by-five card, mix up the cards, and number the backs. Then play a concentration game with the cards and find the ones that match.

comfort   adopt   put dry clothing on a baby
a dozen   legally take someone into your family
change a baby   trade   make more comfortable
need extra hands   twelve   need help
change what you have for what someone else has

Listening

F. Books closed. You are going to the airport to meet a student who will be attending your school. You have never met her before. Listen carefully to her description.

> 1. Kim Young is a 14-year-old Korean girl. She has short, straight, black hair, black eyes, and wears glasses. She is 5 feet tall and weighs 95 pounds. At the airport she will be wearing a blue skirt and a red jacket. She will be wearing a white flower on her jacket.
>
> Now write down three things you will remember about Kim Young so that you will recognize her at the airport.
>
> You are going to pick up your friend's cousin at the airport. Your friend can't go with you, and you have never met the cousin. Listen carefully to the description of the cousin so that you can find him at the airport.
>
> 2. My cousin is 31 years old. He has brown skin like me and brown curly hair. He's very tall and thin, and he's usually smiling or laughing. He will be wearing a white suit and a blue tie at the airport.
>
> Write down four things you will remember about the cousin so that you will recognize him at the airport.

Now open your books and check your answers.

Conversation

G. Discuss the following questions about adoption. You may want to work in groups and then share your discussion with the whole class.

1. Discuss adoption in the United States. For example, who can adopt a child? How much does it cost? (Ask your teacher or other people who might know.)
2. Do you think parents should tell a child that he or she is adopted? Why or why not?
3. Do adopted children and their families have the same kinds of problems as other families?
4. Do adopted children always know who their birth parents are? Why or why not?
5. Do you think adopted children or birth parents should try to find each other? Explain your answer.

Terry McCoy

H. An adopted child wrote each of the following paragraphs. Read each paragraph and discuss how you would answer the child's questions. Before you read, discuss the difference between *parents* and *birth parents*.

1. My name is Tom. I'm 10 years old, and I'm adopted. Sometimes I get so mad at my mom and dad. I think they're mean to me

because I'm adopted. Sometimes I want to say that they can't tell me what to do because they're not my real parents. What should I do?

2. My name is Kim. I'm eight years old, and I'm adopted. I came from Korea, so my skin is brown and I have brown hair and black eyes. My mom and dad both have white skin. Sometimes people ask me stupid questions like, "Why are you a different color from your mom and dad?" These people don't think before they speak. They make me so mad, and they hurt my feelings, too. How should I answer?

3. My name is Ellen, and I'm adopted. I'm 13 years old, and I love my family very much. But I often wonder about my birth mother, and I want to find out more about her. I'm afraid to ask my family to help me because I don't want to hurt their feelings. What should I do?

Writing

I. Choose one child from exercise H and write a short letter to that child. Tell the child what to do and why.

Dear _____,
I know you are wondering what to do. I have some ideas for you. I think you should _____.
_____
_____
The reason is _____
_____
_____. Good luck!

Sincerely,

_____

Skill Builder

J. *Prefixes* are word parts at the beginning of a word. They can change the meaning of a word. For example, the prefix *im-* means "not." The word *impossible* means "not possible." Look at the following prefixes and their meanings. Then, in each blank, write what you think the word means. Compare your answers with another student.

in-	not
pre-	before
re-	again

1. return _____
2. preschool _____
3. inactive _____
4. prepay _____
5. independent _____

6. incomplete _____
7. repay _____
8. prepare _____
9. rewrite _____

More Reading

K. One of the fathers waiting at the airport in Chicago wrote this letter to his new baby. The baby is too young to understand now, but one day his dad will read the letter to him. As you read, think about why the father wrote this letter.

Dear Son,

Today we will meet you for the first time. I want you to know and always remember how important this day is for us, your new parents, who are more excited than ever before in our lives.

We have waited and waited for you to join our family, and finally you are here.

We worked and planned for you for two long years. We saw your picture

before we met you, and we thought you
were beautiful. We began to love you
right away.
    We know that there will be good
times and bad times, easy times
and hard times. But we want you
to know that we, your new parents,
will love you during all those times.
We chose you and we are a family now.

                                    With love,
                                        Dad

Discuss the following.

1. Why did this father write this letter? When will his child read it?
2. Why did these parents work and plan for two years to get their baby?
3. Can you think of anything else this dad should say in this letter?

Extras

L. Use the following books to learn more about adoption.

1. Krementz, Jill. *How It Feels to be Adopted*. Alfred A. Knopf, 1982.
2. Rosenberg, Maxine B. *Being Adopted*. Lothrop, Lee & Shepard, 1984.
3. Sobol, Harriet Langsam. *We Don't Look Like Our Mom and Dad*. Coward, McCann & Geoghegan, 1984.

8

Starting Over: Afghan Families in the U.S.

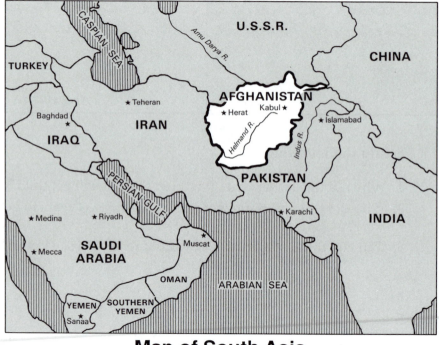

Map of South Asia

Prereading

A. What do you think?

1. What does *starting over* mean?

2. Afghans are people who come from Afghanistan. Where is Afghanistan? Why do you think some Afghans have come to live in the U.S.?

3. What are *traditions*? Why do people want to keep their traditions when they live in a new country?

4. Most Afghans believe in the religion of *Islam*. Share what you know about this religion.

B. What does it mean? In small groups, discuss the meanings of the underlined words. Then use each vocabulary word in a new sentence.

1. It takes a lot of work to keep good family relationships with parents, brothers, sisters, and children. Some families fight and have bad relationships.

2. Immigrants are people who move to a new country and start over. Most immigrants plan to stay in the new country.

3. The majority of the young people are doing well. Most of them enjoy life in the United States.

4. Many people in the world like to wear blue jeans. They are Americanized in their dress.

5. Teachers and parents give lots of advice to children. They always tell kids what to do and how to do it.

Reading

STARTING OVER:
AFGHAN FAMILIES IN THE U.S.

There are many men and women from Afghanistan now living and working in America. They left Afghanistan because a long war made life too difficult and dangerous there. In America, they had to start over. Some Afghans went to big cities like New York and Los Angeles where there were many opportunities for work. They began small businesses or got jobs with family members who were already working. Afghans, like other immigrant groups before them, have worked hard to be successful in the U.S.

Afghan families have changed a lot after coming to

America. For example, many Afghan women have started working outside their homes. They have taken jobs such as salesclerks or bank tellers. Afghan men are glad for the additional income but at the same time they wish their wives were able to spend more time at home like traditional Afghan women.

The majority of the young members of these Afghan families are doing well in the United States. However, as they become more Americanized, they change, and the family relationships change, too. In Afghan society, religion and family have always been very important for all members of a family. But in America, the Afghan teenager becomes very interested in friends, music, and parties, just like young Americans. Afghan parents don't want their children to forget the language, religion and customs of their first country; they don't want their children to become too Americanized. Many adults hope that their religion, Islam, will help their families keep their traditions.

Islam is an important part of everyone's life in Afghanistan, and Afghans in America do not want this to change. For example, when they need to see a doctor, they want a doctor who understands Islam and Afghan traditions. They may not feel comfortable with an American-style doctor's advice. Sometimes, they are not sure they understand the doctor, and they are not sure the doctor understands them.

Starting over isn't always easy. But most Afghans are building a good future for themselves and their children in the U.S. They are working hard in many different ways.

Exercises

Comprehension

C. Answer the following questions about "Starting Over." Revi the underlined words as you discuss the questions.

1. What are two ways that Afghan <u>immigrants</u> get a new start in the United States?
2. Why do Afghan men want their wives to be home more?
3. Young Afghans are becoming <u>Americanized</u>. Give some examples from the story.
4. What worries do Afghans in the U.S. have about their children?
5. What do Afghans think that their religion will help them do?
6. What kind of U.S. doctors do Afghans want? Why are Afghan immigrants uncomfortable with American doctors?

Vocabulary

D. Choose the best definition for each underlined word.

1. Good <u>family relationships</u> are important to most people.
   (a) lots of children
   (b) how people in the family get along with each other
   (c) what kind of work the mother and father do
2. There are more job <u>opportunities</u> in a big city.
   (a) interesting jobs
   (b) well-paid jobs
   (c) chances for a job
3. My father always gives me lots of <u>advice</u>.
   (a) money
   (b) telling me what I should do
   (c) food
4. Afghans hope to keep their <u>traditions</u>.
   (a) ways of doing things, or religion
   (b) good behavior
   (c) good luck
5. The <u>majority</u> of the young people are doing well.
   (a) a few
   (b) all
   (c) most
6. Religion is important for all <u>members</u> of an Afghan family.
   (a) people who belong to the family
   (b) males
   (c) children

7. Afghan men are glad for the additional <u>income</u>.
   (a) hours of work
   (b) money you can earn from a job
   (c) food

Listening

E. Books closed. You will hear a short discussion, "Women's Work." Then you will be asked three questions about it.

WOMEN'S WORK

American women have always worked hard. Traditionally, most American mothers worked only at home or on the family farm. It was their job to take care of the children and the house, feed their families, and help with the farm work.

Now, many American mothers also work outside the home. Life is expensive in the U.S., and families need this money. More women study and have professions. They need and want to work outside the home.

Because of this, the traditional American family has changed. Many young children now go to child-care centers while their parents work. Little children spend much less time with their parents than before. Sometimes, young children come home after school and are alone until their parents come home from work. These children must take care of themselves. Many husbands must help with the cleaning, the cooking, and the baby-sitting because there is no one at home during the day to do this work. The lives of all the people in the family have changed.

Now write the answers to the following questions. Then open your books to check your answers.

1. Traditionally, where did American women work?

2. Why do many American women work outside the home now?

3. How has the American family changed because so many women now work outside the home? (Give two examples.)

Conversation

F. In small groups, discuss the following questions. Then share your ideas with the whole class.

1. How do you feel about women working both inside and outside of the home?
2. If a woman has a job and a family, should her husband share equally in the work at home? Why or why not? If so, what jobs should the man do at home?
3. What do you think about young children going to child-care centers while their parents work?
4. What do you think about young children taking care of themselves at home?

Writing

G. What changes did you have to make when you moved to the U.S.? Think about changes in family, school, jobs, religion, and so forth. Then write a paragraph about one of these changes. When you finish, share your writing with another student.

When I came to the U.S., the biggest change I had to make was

_____

_____.

This change was _____ because _____
(easy/difficult)

_____

_____.

Now this _____ a problem for me because _____
(is/isn't)

_____

_____.

Skill Builder

H. Discuss the following.

1. When people come to a new culture, they have to learn new *body language* and *gestures*. In the U.S., what is the gesture to say *yes* (without words)? How about *no*?

2. Think about some other gestures that you often see here. Think of at least five and talk about their meanings. Are there any that you should be very careful about using?

3. With a partner, talk about some gestures from your language and culture. Can you think of any that have a different meaning in your culture and in the U.S.? Share your answers with the class.

4. At home, watch TV and look for gestures that Americans often use. Discuss what you saw.

More Reading

I. Many newspapers have an advice column where someone answers letters from readers. Read the following letters to Ms. Helpful and then write an answer to each.

Dear Ms. Helpful,

I am a 16-year-old high school student. I came here from Afghanistan in 1986. My parents and I like living in the United States, but sometimes we don't agree about *how* to live here. For example, my parents usually want me to stay home and study, even when my friends are at the movies or at a party. I don't know how long I can keep my friends if I never see them! Also, I had a job after school, but then I started getting bad grades. My parents said I had to quit my job. So now I have no friends and no money. I am trying hard to start a life in the U.S., but my parents are making it harder. What should I do?

Signed,
Unhappy in L.A.

Dear Unhappy in L.A.,

I can think of a few different things to try. One is _____ _____.

Another is _____ _____.

And the third is _____ _____.

Don't give up!

Ms. Helpful

Dear Ms. Helpful,

My husband and I came to the U.S. about two years ago. At first, it was OK. We were homesick and we didn't know how to live here, but we tried. Now I think my husband wants to go back to Afghanistan. He has a job here, but he doesn't like it. I can understand how he feels; he used to be a government official, and now he drives a taxi in the city. I worry a lot about our life here, but I worry about returning to our country, too. What should we do?

Signed,
Worried

Dear Worried,

You need to find out about _____ _____ _____.

Then talk about _____ _____ _____ _____.

Maybe you can talk to _____ about your decision.

Good luck!
Ms. Helpful

Extras

J. Use the following books to learn more about Afghanistan and the immigrant experience in the U.S.

1. Ashabranner, Brent. *The New Americans: Changing Patterns in U.S. Immigration.* Dodd, Mead, 1983.

2. Ashabranner, Brent, and Melissa Ashabranner. *Into a Strange Land: Unaccompanied Refugee Youth in America.* Dodd, Mead, 1987.

3. Clifford, Mary Louise. *The Land and People of Afghanistan.* J.B. Lippincott, 1989.

4. Perrin, Linda. *Coming to America: Immigrants from the Far East.* Delacorte, 1980.

5. Santoli, Al. *New Americans, an Oral History.* Viking Penguin, 1988.

9

Olympic Stars

AP/Wide World Photos

Prereading

A. What do you think?

1. What are the Olympic Games? How often are they played?
2. Do you remember seeing or hearing about any Olympic Games? When and where were they?

3. Make a list of some Olympic sports.

<table>
<tr><td></td><td>**Sports at
Summer Games**</td><td>**Sports at
Winter Games**</td></tr>
<tr><td>Example:</td><td><u>Swimming</u></td><td><u>ice hockey</u></td></tr>
</table>

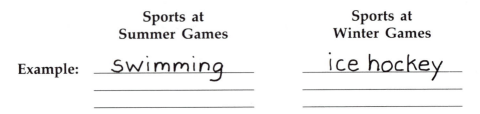

4. In what section of the newspaper could you read about the Olympics?

5. The next reading is a newspaper story about diving at the 1988 Olympics. Before reading the story, look at the picture of diving. Discuss the difference between *platform diving* and *springboard diving*.

B. What does it mean? Find a word (or phrase) on the right that means the same as the word (or phrase) on the left. Write the letter in the blank.

____	1. a person who helps someone practice for a sport	a.	a diver
		b.	to beat
		c.	competition
____	2. profession	d.	a coach
____	3. what you win if you get first place in the Olympic Games	e.	a worker
		f.	a gold medal
		g.	career
		h.	to get stitches
____	4. to get a better score than another person or team		
____	5. a race or game to see which person or team wins		
____	6. a person who dives		
____	7. to have a doctor close a cut in the skin by sewing		

Reuters/Bettmann Newsphotos

Greg Louganis

Reading

DIVER GREG LOUGANIS WINS
TWO GOLD MEDALS

SEOUL, KOREA. Greg Louganis won his second gold medal today. In his last dive of the 1988 Olympics diving competition, Louganis beat Chinese diver, Xiong Ni, by only one point. "It was probably the biggest and most difficult dive of Greg's life," said his diving coach.

Louganis, who has competed in three Olympics, has not had an easy time here in Seoul. First, he arrived with a sore shoulder. He then got a sore throat and a fever, which worried him. Greg's coach was worried, too, because Greg wasn't eating well and he never wanted to leave his hotel room.

A few days later, in the first diving competition, Louganis jumped high into the air and began his first dive perfectly. But then he came crashing down and hit his head on the diving board. He cut his head and had to get five stitches. This didn't stop Greg. Thirty minutes later, he returned to the pool and made the best dive of the day. Just one day later, he won the gold medal in the 3-meter board competition.

Today in the final diving competition, the divers had to do 10 dives from a 10-meter platform. After the first four dives, Greg had the most points. Later, the young Chinese diver, Xiong Ni, (who is 14 years old—exactly half the age of Louganis) began to lead. On the tenth and final dive, Louganis was three points behind Xiong. Louganis knew he had to do a perfect dive to beat Xiong. He had to jump well off the board, fly high in the air, keep his body in the correct form, and enter the water without a splash. He also knew that this was his most difficult dive of the day. As he stood on the platform before the dive, he thought, "It doesn't matter what happens; my mother will still love me."

The dive was perfect. When Louganis came out of the water, he knew he had won the competition. The crowd roared. His coach was dancing and crying on the side of the pool. Greg began to cry, too. "I wasn't crying because I won the gold medal. I was crying because I knew that this was my last Olympic competition."

Now that the Games are over, Louganis will begin a new career. He plans to become an actor. Most actors dream of being a star one day, but Greg Louganis is already a star—an Olympic star.

Exercises

Comprehension

C. A news story always answers the following questions:

Who did something? _____

What did the person do? _____

When did the person do it? _____

Where did it happen? _____

How did it happen? _____

On each of the preceding lines, write a short answer about the Greg Louganis story. Compare your answers with another student.

D. Discuss the following questions.

1. Why were the two weeks before the Seoul Olympic Diving Competition difficult for Greg Louganis? Give three reasons.

2. The cut on his head didn't stop Louganis. What did he do after he got the cut?
3. How old was Greg Louganis at the time of the 1988 Olympics?
4. Why did Louganis need a perfect dive to beat Xiong Ni?
5. How did Louganis know he had won the gold medal?
6. Why did he begin to cry after he had won?
7. What does Greg plan to do after the Games?

Vocabulary

E. Discuss the meanings of the underlined words in the following sentences. Then answer the questions about each word or phrase.

1. Louganis was three points behind.
   If Xiong had 10 points, how many did Louganis have?

   _____

   _____

2. It doesn't matter what happens. My mother will still love me. What are some other times that you might say, "It doesn't matter"?

   _____

   _____

3. The crowd roared.
   What animal roars? _____

   _____

4. Then he got a sore throat and a fever.
   What is a normal body temperature? _____

   _____

5. He must jump well off the board, fly high in the air, keep his body <u>in the correct form</u>, and enter the water without a <u>splash</u>. What are four important parts of a dive?

_____

_____

6. He plans to become an <u>actor</u>. He is already a <u>star</u>. Are all actors stars? (Explain your answer.)

_____

_____

Listening

F. Books closed. Listen to each of the following radio news stories about sports. You will hear each story two times. After the second time, answer *who, what, when, where, why,* and *how* questions about each story.

1. At Tuesday's Olympic Games in Korea, there was a big surprise in the men's 200-meter swim race. Duncan Armstrong, an Australian swimmer, won the gold medal. He also set a new world record for the fastest time in the 200-meter race. No one expected him to win, but he beat three of the world's best swimmers.

   Now write your answers to the following questions.
   (a) Who?
   (b) What?
   (c) When?
   (d) Where?

2. It was a tough week for the U.S. Volleyball team because it played against Brazil and the Soviet Union. However, the U.S. team beat the Soviet team on Sunday, and received its second gold medal. After this, many people have described the U.S. team as the best ever in volleyball.

Now answer the following questions.
  (a) Who?
  (b) What?
  (c) When?
  (d) Where?

3. Debi Thomas, a black American figureskater, surprised the world by announcing her recent marriage. Debi was secretly married just before the 1988 Winter Olympics. Debi, who plans to be a doctor, will live in California with her new husband. There she will study and continue to skate.

Now answer the following questions.
  (a) Who?
  (b) What?
  (c) How?
  (d) When?

4. Speedskater Dan Jansen planned to win two gold medals at the 1988 Winter Olympics in Calgary, Canada. However, he had some bad luck. Dan fell after having a poor start in his first race. Then, just as he was about to win his second race, he fell again. Dan said he may try again for the gold in another Olympics.

Now answer the following questions.
  (a) Who?
  (b) What?
  (c) When?
  (d) Where?

Conversation

G. Discuss the following questions about sports.

1. Are there some people in your class who enjoy sports a lot? Why do they like sports so much? Do they like to play or watch? What sports do they like?
2. What's the most exciting sport to watch? What's the most exciting sport to play? Explain your answers.

3. Are most sports dangerous? Why is diving dangerous? Can you think of dangers in some other Olympic sports?

4. How do you think the divers feel as they stand at the top of the platform, waiting to dive? How do you think Louganis felt, knowing that he had to make a perfect dive?

5. Many people believe that sports are beautiful to watch. What do you think and why?

6. It takes many years of hard work to get ready for the Olympics. Why do athletes want to work so hard and so long?

7. Do you know anyone who enters sports competition? Why do they do it?

8. Would you like to compete in a sport? Why or why not? Would you feel nervous in a competition? Why or why not?

H. Ask some classmates to explain how they play their favorite sports. They can bring some *sports equipment* to class and talk about it.

Skill Builder

I. Follow these steps to interview a class visitor.

1. Invite someone to come to your class for an interview. Choose someone you really want to meet—an athlete, a police officer, an artist, for example.

2. Before the interview, work together to make a list of all the questions to ask.

3. During the interview, each person must ask at least one question.

4. Take notes during the interview. You will use them later to write a story about the person you interview.

Writing

J. Organize the notes from your interview and use them to write two paragraphs about the person. First, look at your notes to find ways to describe him. Then write a first paragraph, telling at least three things about the person.

Look back at your notes to find two or three interesting things the visitor said. Underline the words you can use. Then write a second paragraph.

Begin your paragraphs like this:

On ____ (date) _____, we interviewed

_____. _____

_____

_____

_____

_____.

One thing that I thought was really interesting about

_____ is _____.

_____

_____.

After writing, share paragraphs with other class members.

More Reading

K. Before reading the interview with Olympic speedskater Mary Docter, do the vocabulary exercise.

Find a sentence on the right that means the same as a sentence on the left. Pay attention to the underlined words. Write the correct letter in the blank.

___	1. You have to <u>train</u> hard.	a.	He moves well with the music.
___	2. I liked the book <u>right from the beginning</u>.	b.	I liked it right away.
___	3. I met him <u>by accident</u>.	c.	You have to practice hard.
___	4. This is <u>serious</u>.	d.	I didn't plan to meet him, but I did.
___	5. He has good <u>rhythm</u>.	e.	This isn't funny.

John Biever/All Sport

Mary Docter

Reading

MARY DOCTER, OLYMPIAN

Mary Docter has been a member of the United States Olympic Speedskating Team three times—in 1980, 1984, and 1988. Mary says that she became a skater by accident. She lived next to a lake in Madison, Wisconsin, and in the winter she just skated for fun. One winter she skated with two neighbors who were good speedskaters, Eric and Beth Heiden. Mary knew right away that she wanted to be a speedskater, too.

Being a serious speedskater was a lot of hard work for Mary. After school each day, she made a two-hour drive to Milwaukee, where she practiced for about four hours before driving back to Madison. Usually, Mary left school at 12:30 P.M. and returned home at about 8:30 P.M.

Mary finished high school in four years. Then she began training and racing more and more. She skated and took college classes for the next nine years. She finally graduated with a degree in science education. Because of skating, Mary missed a lot of fun with her school friends, but she says she never really wanted to do anything but skate. Mary even enjoys training. Sometimes she listens to a Michael Jackson tape while she practices. "Michael Jackson helps me skate with rhythm," she says.

Skating has opened many doors for Mary. She has traveled to Europe to skate 10 different times, and she has met some famous people, including two U.S. presidents. Today, Mary is studying to be a physician's assistant. She says, "No matter what, I will never hang up my skates!"

Exercises

Comprehension

L. Answer the following questions about "Mary Docter, Olympian."

1. How did Mary learn to skate?
2. How much did Mary practice?
3. Did Mary think school was important, too? How do you know?
4. Why does Mary sometimes listen to music when she practices?
5. How did skating <u>open doors</u> for Mary?
6. Mary says, "I will never hang up my skates." What does she mean?

M. Work in groups of three to write endings for the following sentences. When you are finished, share your sentences with the other groups.

1. To be a really good athlete, you must . . .
2. Mary missed a lot of fun, but . . .
3. Some of the things Mary has done because of skating are . . .

Extras

N. Use the following books or videos to learn more about the Olympics.

1. Aaseng, Nathan. *Eric Heiden, Winner in Gold*. Lerner, 1980.
2. Fradin, Dennis B. *Olympics*. Regensteiner Publishing Enterprises, Inc., 1983.
3. Glubok, Shirley. *Olympic Games in Ancient Greece*. Harper & Row, 1976.
4. Tatlow, Peter. *The Olympics*.
5. Yalouris, Nicolaos, ed. *The Eternal Olympics*. Caratxas Brothers Publishers, 1979.

10

Could It Be A UFO?

Prereading

A. What do you think?

1. What do you think the words *unidentified flying object* (UFO) mean?

2. Discuss the preceding picture. What is the object in the sky? Describe it.

3. Where do you think the object came from?

4. In the U.S., when people see a UFO, they tell the police. Why? Is it the same in your country?

5. Look at the following story. How can you tell it is a newspaper story?

6. The following story is about UFOs. Look at the headline (title) of the story. Make some guesses about what the story will be about.

B. What does it mean? Guess the meanings of the underlined words in the following sentences.

1. We live on the <u>planet</u> earth.

2. This is really a strange <u>creature</u>. I don't know what kind of animal it is.

3. Only <u>humans</u> can speak languages with thousands of words. Animals cannot.

4. The light on the top of the police car is <u>flashing</u>; the red light is turning around and around quickly.

5. This plant has no name. It is <u>unidentified</u>.

6. The <u>traffic</u> at rush hour is always the worst. Everyone is driving to work at the same time, and there are too many cars on the road.

Reading

UFOs IN BELLEVILLE?

BELLEVILLE, WI—Are strange creatures coming to Belleville? Maybe not, but some people here are seeing flashing, colored lights and strange objects in the sky. What are these unidentified flying objects?

On January 15, policemen in Belleville watched five lights flashing in the sky for six hours. Someone at a nearby airport saw the same lights.

There was another sighting like this in Belleville on March 6. Harry

Roberts and his friend were coming home from work when they saw an egg-shaped object in the sky. There were five smaller objects behind it. "I remember it so well," said Roberts. "It was so close and so big. There wasn't any sound at all."

Don Smith, who studies UFOs in Chicago, came to Belleville to check out these reports. He said the lights were not from airplanes. "I checked all airplane traffic for that day and there were no planes near Belleville at that time," he said.

The people of Belleville, a small farm town, learned more about UFOs at a town meeting with Mr. Smith. Smith said, "Most people see UFOs in small towns or in the country," He also said that sometimes people see strange creatures in the UFOs.

What do the people of Belleville think about the UFOs? A few people are worried that creatures from another planet might be coming to their town to study humans. Most people just want more information about the strange objects. One man said, "I don't think they were UFOs. I don't believe in creatures from another planet."

Exercises

Comprehension

C. Discuss the following.

1. Where is Belleville?
2. Look at the first two paragraphs of the newspaper story again. Ask and answer questions about the paragraphs using the following words:
   (a) Who?
   (b) What?
   (c) Where?
   (d) When?
3. What did the policemen see?
4. What did Harry Roberts and his friend see?
5. Who is Don Smith? Why did he come to Belleville?
6. What do most people in Belleville think about the UFOs?

7. What does one person (at the end of the story) think about the UFOs?

8. What do you think these people saw in the sky? Work together to make a list of possibilities.

D. Write *T* for true and *F* for false.

____ 1. The policemen saw the lights of airplanes in the sky.
____ 2. Harry Roberts and his friend heard strange noises in the sky on January 15.
____ 3. Don Smith studies UFOs.
____ 4. Most people see UFOs in the city.
____ 5. Some people see strange creatures in the UFOs.
____ 6. Everyone thinks that there are strange creatures coming to Belleville to study humans.

Vocabulary

E. Read the following sentences and discuss the meanings of the underlined words.

1. Don Smith came to Belleville to <u>check out</u> these <u>reports</u>.
2. There was another <u>sighting</u> in Belleville on March 6.
3. They saw an <u>egg-shaped object</u> in the sky.
4. The people learned more about UFOs at a <u>town meeting</u>.
5. Most people just want more <u>information</u>.
6. I don't <u>believe in</u> creatures from another planet.

Listening

F. Books closed. Listen to the following conversation. Chris and Steve are talking about life on other planets. After the conversation, you will be asked questions about what Chris believes.

> *Chris:* What do you think about life on other planets?
> *Steve:* I don't know. I suppose it's possible. How about you? Do you think there are living things up there?
> *Chris:* I really doubt it. How could anything live on those planets? There's no air and no water.

Steve: You never know. Maybe there are different kinds of creatures that don't need air or water.

Chris: Do you really believe that? I suppose you also think that UFOs come from other planets?

Steve: Yes, I do. Where else could they come from?

Chris: UFOs are probably just some kind of airplanes that the government uses for experiments.

Steve: Oh sure! Then why doesn't the government tell us about it?

Chris: Maybe they're doing *secret* experiments or something they don't want us to know about.

Steve: Well, just remember that we sent men to the moon, so why couldn't other planets send their people here?

Chris: I don't think I'll believe it until I see it with my own eyes.

Work with a partner and write your answers to the following questions as your teacher reads them aloud. Then look back at Chris and Steve's conversation and check your answers.

1. What are Chris and Steve arguing about?
2. Write two reasons why Chris believes there is no life on other planets.
3. Read the conversation aloud, and check your answers while you read.

Conversation

G. In newspaper stories, some sentences are *facts* and some are *opinions*.

Example: *The population of Belleville is 5,000.*
This is a *fact*. It isn't what someone thinks, it is actual information.
I don't believe in UFOs.
This is an *opinion*. It is what someone thinks about something.

1. With a partner, read the following sentences. Decide if the sentence is *fact* or *opinion*, and write your choice on the line. Write *F* for fact and *O* for opinion.

____ a. There are 365 days in a year.
____ b. There are too many students in this class.

___ c. Creatures live on other planets.
___ d. It's easy to live in the U.S.
___ e. The president of the U.S. is elected for four years.
___ f. The cost of housing in this town is too high.
___ g. That car costs $6,850.
___ h. The U.S. sent men to the moon in 1969.

2. Look back at the story "UFOs in Belleville." Find some examples of fact and some examples of opinion.

Writing

H. Work together and write some facts and opinions about the town or city where you live.

Facts about _____
                    (your town/city)
  1.

  2.

  3.

Opinions about _____
                    (your town/city)
  1.

  2.

  3.

Now work independently and write some facts and opinions about another topic. Choose from: your school, your ESL class, your work, your country, and so forth.

Facts about _____
                    (topic you choose)
  1.

  2.

  3.

My opinions about _____
                    (same topic)
  1.

  2.

  3.

I. The following is a phone conversation between a woman who saw a UFO and a police officer. Work in pairs to finish writing the conversation. Then read it to the class.

Woman:　I want to report a UFO.
Officer:　Where did you see this?
Woman:　_____

Officer:　What did it look like?
Woman:　_____
　　　　　_____

Officer:　Did you see anything inside the UFO?
Woman:　_____
　　　　　_____

Officer:　We'll be right over to check it out.

Skill Builder

J. Bring some newspapers to class. Look at some of the headlines, and then discuss the following questions.

1. What is a headline? Is it a complete sentence? Why or why not?
2. Why are headlines important to a newspaper reader?

K. Work in pairs and read the following newspaper headlines. Write what you think the story under the headline is going to be about. Discuss your answers with the class.

Example A:　PROBLEMS IN U.S. CITIES GROW
What will be in the story? *Problems like crime and drugs are getting bigger in US cities*

1. 14 BILLION HUMANS BY 2100?

　_____
　_____

2. DRINKING AGE CHANGES AGAIN

　_____
　_____

3. 8-YEAR-OLD SAVES BABY

_____

_____

4. THREE HURT IN CAR ACCIDENT

_____

_____

More Reading

L. Read the following true story. Be ready to answer some questions about the story. Before you read, discuss the following words and phrases.

actor   New Jersey
on the air   to be in a panic
an announcer   Mars
to interrupt   spaceship
a play   foolish

AN UNUSUAL "NEWS PROGRAM"

Halloween night in 1938 was one of the strangest Halloweens in history. Some people enjoyed the holiday by going to parties or trick-or-treating. Many others, unfortunately, stayed home to listen to a frightening radio program. During this program, a group of actors read a radio play on the air. The name of the play was "The War of the Worlds."

The radio actors read the play as if it were a true story. The play started with some dance music. Then an announcer said, "We interrupt this program for a special news bulletin from New Jersey." The announcer told how a large, round, yellowish-white spaceship from Mars had landed on a farm in New Jersey. The reporters said that there were snake-like creatures coming out of the spaceship. They said that the creatures were killing people everywhere.

Most of the people who were listening to the radio thought the news program was real. They didn't hear the first part, which said that it was just a play. All over the country, people who listened to the play ran into the streets screaming and shouting. They thought the world was coming to an end. Some people got in their cars to drive away, but they didn't know where to go. Traffic was tied up for miles in many cities. Hundreds of people called the police and newspapers; all the telephone lines were busy. Movie theaters, churches, and restaurants began to close. People were in a panic.

Later, radio announcers told everyone that it was just a play, that it wasn't real. People felt foolish and were angry at the radio station. Everywhere people asked the question, "Why did everyone believe this story? Why did everyone panic?"

Comprehension

Work in groups of three and discuss the following questions. One person in each group writes the answers. Then discuss your answers with the entire class.

1. When did the radio station put the play on the radio?
2. Was the radio play true?
3. Describe the spaceship in the play.
4. Describe the creatures that came out of the spaceship. What did they do to the people?
5. Write down three things that people did when they heard the play.
6. How did people feel when they found out that it was not true?
7. Why do you and your group members think people panicked when they heard this play? (Give at least two reasons.)

Extras

M. Use the following books or videos to learn more about UFOs.

1. Berger, Melvin. *UFOs, E.T.s, and Visitors from Space.* G.P. Putnam, 1988.
2. Branley, Franklyn. *Is There Life in Outer Space?* Harper & Row, 1984.
3. Rutland, Jonathon. *UFO's.* Random House, 1987.
4. Spielberg, Steven D., director. *E.T. the Extraterrestrial.* Ambin Entertainment, N.C.A., 1982.
5. Wilson, Ben. *UFO's.* The Bookwright Press, 1989.

11

The Woman of His Dreams

Prereading

A. What do you think? Bring some newspapers to class to help you discuss the following questions.

1. Do you read the newspaper? Why or why not?

2. Look at the newspapers you brought to class. Identify some of the newspaper *sections*. Which parts look the most interesting?

3. In what section of the newspaper can you find the "Help Wanted" ads, also known as want ads?

4. How can want ads help you? *Skim* (read very quickly) some want ads. Make a list of things people might buy or sell in the want ads.

5. Read the following ads from the Personal section of the want ads. Then discuss why people put Personal ads in the newspaper.

LONELY? Young, active university student needs friend. Interested in tennis, volleyball, studying engineering. Call 233-9086.

DATE WANTED: Handsome young male has two tickets for theater 9/22. Looking for intelligent, attractive woman who enjoys theater, good food, and good conversation. Call 233-8467.

B. What does it mean? Fill in the blanks with the following words to complete each sentence.

used   columns   air conditioner
voice   scanned

1. I bought a _____ car yesterday. It isn't new, but it's in good condition.

2. It was 96 degrees Fahrenheit yesterday, so we decided to turn on the _____.

3. When I listen to myself talking on a cassette tape, my _____ always sounds very strange.

4. Newspaper stories are written in _____, so you read down the page instead of just across.

5. He turned the magazine pages quickly and _____ the stories. Later, he read one or two of the stories he was interested in.

Reading

THE WOMAN OF HIS DREAMS

On a sunny Saturday in early June, Craig Peterson woke up in an apartment that was already as hot as an oven. It was very uncomfortable, and he knew it would be worse by the end of the day. "I've either got to move or buy an air conditioner," Craig thought to himself. He decided to go out for breakfast.

The restaurant down the street from his apartment was pleasantly cool. Craig sat down to enjoy a nice long breakfast with the morning paper. He opened the newspaper to the want ads; he thought he might find a used air conditioner there. However, as he scanned the columns, one of the ads in the Personal section caught his eye:

> WANTED: TRAVEL writer wants driver/friend, age 25–35, who enjoys sports, reading, traveling, cooking. Call L. Bunker 632-8471.

Craig read the ad again: sports, reading, traveling, cooking—all things that interested him. "That's me," thought Craig. "Someone out there is looking for me! I'm the right age, I enjoy all those things, and I can drive."

He went to the phone and dialed 632-8471. A gentle, female voice answered, "Hello."

"Hello," began Craig. "I'm calling about the ad in the paper."

"Yes," said the lovely voice. "Are you interested?"

"Uh . . . well, I think so. . . . I mean, yes!" answered Craig nervously. That voice! Who did it belong to? L. Bunker . . . Linda? Laurie? Lynn? Was the travel writer a beautiful young woman?

"It's important to find someone as soon as possible. Could you come to 1421 Windsor Road at 5:30 this evening?" asked the voice.

"I'd love to," answered Craig. "I'll see you then."

To be continued . . .

Exercises

Comprehension

C. Answer the following questions about the story.

1. Make some guesses about Craig. How old is he? What does he look like? What does he do every day?
2. Why was Craig looking at the want ads?
3. What kind of ad did Craig find?
4. What kind of person was the travel writer looking for?
5. Why did Craig call the telephone number in the ad?
6. What kind of voice answered the phone?
7. Why did Craig think her name might be Lynn, Linda, or Laurie?
8. When will Craig meet L. Bunker?

D. Discuss the following.

1. What does the ad tell you about L. Bunker?
2. How can you tell Craig was nervous on the phone? Why do you think he was nervous?
3. Think about the title, "The Woman of His Dreams." What do you think this means?
4. Guess who L. Bunker is. Describe the person.
5. What do you think will happen at the meeting between Craig and L. Bunker?

Vocabulary

E. Read the following sentences. Explain the underlined words or phrases.

1. His apartment <u>was as hot as an oven</u>.
2. Craig was feeling <u>uncomfortable</u>.
3. The restaurant was <u>pleasantly</u> cool.
4. He read the ads until something <u>caught his eye</u>.
5. It's important to find someone <u>as soon as possible</u>.

Listening

F. Books closed. Listen to the following conversation between a person who is calling about a want ad and a person who is trying to sell an air conditioner. After the conversation you will be asked questions about the air conditioner and its price.

Conversation:

Buyer: I'm calling about your ad in the paper for the used air conditioner.

Seller: Great, do you have any questions?

Buyer: Yes, is it in good condition?

Seller: Oh, yes. It's in excellent condition. It's only one year old.

Buyer: Why are you selling it?

Seller: We're moving across the country, and we just don't have room to take it.

Buyer: How much are you asking for the air conditioner?

Seller: We're asking $350.

Buyer: Oh, that's more than I want to pay. How about $200?

Seller: I'll think about it. Why don't you come look at it, and we can discuss it?

Buyer: OK. I'll be there in about half an hour.

Seller: See you then.

Now write your answers to the following questions as your teacher reads them aloud. Then open your book and check your answers.

Questions:

1. Describe the used air conditioner. Tell two things about it.
2. Why does the person want to sell the air conditioner?
3. What does the buyer think about the price?
4. Will the seller change the price? Why or why not?

Conversation

G. Read and discuss the following want ads. Talk about any vocabulary you don't know. Then, in groups of three, answer the questions about the ads.

USED CARS FOR SALE	**DELIVERY DRIVER NEEDED**
CHEVY Monza '79. Good body. Needs tires. Great winter car. $800. 424–3582 after 6PM.	Female/male energetic person for local delivery. Must have excellent driving record. Will train. Full-time days. 986–5532.
VW Rabbit '80, 2 door very clean inside & out, new brakes and tires, no rust. $1500/best offer, 986–8449.	**UNFURNISHED APARTMENTS** BRIDGE ROAD—3/4 bedroom, only $600, includes heat, free parking, laundry. 986–3883.
JOBS FARM HELP WANTED Experience. References. Housing Available. No pets. 986–0987.	JOHNSTON ST.—1 bedroom, $360, includes utilities. No kids, no pets. On bus line. 986–0098.
CHILD-CARE WORKER Part-time, $3.75/hour to start, nonsmoker. 986–0754.	RIVER RD.—2 bedroom, clean, $400, with heat. Near schools and bus. 986–7751.

Answer the following questions about the ads.

1. Which ad will you answer if you need a part-time job?
2. You need a job, but you have no experience. What ads can you answer?
3. Which used car is the best buy? Why?

4. If you buy the Chevy Monza, what do you need to do after you buy it?

5. You need an unfurnished apartment. You and your wife have one daughter, who is of school age. Which apartment is best for you?

6. You need an unfurnished apartment. You and your husband have two children, a dog, and a car. Which apartment is best for you?

Skill Builder

H. Work in groups of two. Fill in the blanks to write your own want ads.

BABYSITTER WANTED for __
_____-year-old child. Must be
_____. $_____ per
hour. _____ 321–8875.

FURNISHED APARTMENT

_____ bedrooms. _____ in-
cluded. Near _____.
No _____. $_____
per month. Call 276–9908.

FOR SALE: _____
_____
_____
_____

PERSONAL
_____
_____
_____
_____

I. Look at the want ad section of the newspaper. In your next class, talk about one interesting ad that you read.

Writing

J. Look back to the questions in comprehension exercise D. <u>Before you read</u> the following conclusion, write your own ending to the story, "The Woman of His Dreams." Begin like this:

At 5:30 that evening, Craig was standing in front of the address on Windsor Road. _____

_____

_____

_____ . . .

More Reading

K. Before you read the ending of the story, choose the best answer to each of the following questions.

   1. You want to introduce one person to another. What will you say?
     (a) I'm glad to meet you.
     (b) I'm fine.
     (c) I'd like you to meet _____.

   2. You just met Mrs. Green, your new neighbor. What will you say?
     (a) Fine, thank you.
     (b) Glad to meet you.
     (c) Yes, thank you.

Now choose the word or words that mean the same as the underlined word or words.

   3. My grandmother was a wonderful person. She had a gentle voice and <u>warm</u> eyes.
     (a) violet-colored eyes
     (b) friendly eyes
     (c) her eyes were closed

4. He <u>dropped everything</u> and went to their house.
   (a) everything fell on the floor
   (b) ran as fast as he could
   (c) stopped doing what he had been doing

5. He felt <u>silly</u>.
   (a) foolish
   (b) comfortable
   (c) hot

6. <u>What do you have in mind?</u>
   (a) What's wrong with you?
   (b) What are you thinking?
   (c) What did you ask me?

THE WOMAN OF HIS DREAMS (Continued)

At 5:30, Craig was standing in front of the house at 1421 Windsor Road. He was feeling a little silly about dropping everything to find out about the ad. Then the door opened, and the most wonderful eyes Craig had ever seen looked out. "Mr. Peterson?" asked the voice.

She let him in. She had dark hair, warm eyes, and a soft smile. Craig melted. This was the woman of his dreams. He heard her say, "I'd like you to meet Mr. L. Bunker, my father. Dad, this is Craig Peterson, who is answering your newspaper ad."

Craig's eyes turned toward the sofa in the living room. He saw a man about 60 years old with the same soft, warm eyes as the young woman.

"Glad to meet you, Mr. Peterson," said the man. "I'm looking for a young man to travel around the U.S. with me this summer and help out with the driving. I'm getting too old to do all the driving myself, and the days get long when you're traveling all alone. My daughter here used to go with me, but this summer she is too busy with her own work to be with me all the time. She has promised to join us for a few weeks during the summer, though."

Craig was too surprised to speak. L. Bunker wasn't this young woman. It was her father!

"Well, Mr. Peterson . . . what do you say?" asked

Mr. L. Bunker. "Are you interested in talking about this?"

Craig thought carefully. His eyes went from the father to the young woman. He remembered what the father had said about the daughter joining them for a few weeks. He began to smile. "Yes, I'm interested," said Craig. "Let's find out exactly what you have in mind."

As he sat down next to L. Bunker, Craig remembered his hot apartment and the air conditioner. He probably wouldn't need either one this summer!

Comprehension

Discuss the following questions about the ending of the story.

1. Describe the woman who answered the door.
2. Craig "melted" means that he _____.
3. Who is L. Bunker? What is the surprise ending of this story?
4. Why does L. Bunker want a driver/friend?
5. Do you think Craig will take the job? Why or why not?
6. Do you think "The Woman of His Dreams" is a good title for this story? Why or why not?

Extras

L. Read more love stories and poetry in the following books.

1. Borisoff, Norman. *Betwitched and Bewildered*. Dell Publishing Co., 1983.
2. ESL adaptations of O. Henry's *The Gift of the Magi*.
3. Ritchie, Jean. *Apple Seeds and Soda Straws, Some Love Charms and Legends*. Henry Z. Walck, Inc., 1965.

12
Tornado

Prereading

A. What do you think?

1. The preceding picture shows a *tornado*. What is the shape of the
   tornado? How does it move? What happens when a tornado hits
   the ground?

2. Describe a *storm* you have seen, either here or in your country. Make a list of words that describe storms.

3. The reading in this chapter is a *feature* story, similar to one in a newspaper. To learn about feature stories, bring in several newspapers. Find the *features section* of each newspaper. What is it called? What kinds of stories does the section have? What other kinds of readings are there in this section?

B. What does it mean? As you read "Tornado," look for the following phrases. When you finish reading, work in pairs to explain what the phrases mean. Then share your ideas with another group.

severe thunderstorm
bright lightning
an unbelievable miracle

whistling wind
the pressure of the roaring wind

Reading

TORNADO
by John Miller
for the Barneveld Times

On the night of June 8, my life changed forever. Before that night, I was just a 17-year-old high school student living in a small Wisconsin town. I worried about things like soccer games, algebra, and having enough money to go out with my friends. After that night, I had bigger things to think about.

The night of June 8, I was watching a late-night TV show with my family. We got a little nervous when the TV news said that there might be a severe thunderstorm. But there are often bad storms in June, so we all watched the end of the TV show and went to bed.

Soon after we went to sleep, I woke up and saw bright lightning in the sky. It was so bright that the whole room turned white. I heard a sound that was like a hundred jets flying past the house. I had never heard such a noise in all my life. My ears hurt from the strange whistle.

Suddenly, even stranger things started happening. I could feel the heavy pressure of the roaring wind. The whole house began to shake, and the floor under me seemed to fall away. I knew I should get to the basement, but it was too late. I held onto my bed as I felt myself falling into the darkness.

After ten minutes, the tornado was over. I was so frightened I couldn't move. When I finally opened my eyes, everything was dark and it was raining hard. I could hear people shouting. I began to look for my family. I found Mom and Dad lying under some pieces of wood. They were alive and not badly hurt. It was an unbelievable miracle. My sisters had cuts, but they were OK too—another miracle.

We climbed outside and heard people calling for help. There was still lightning and a warm, whistling wind, but no rain. By 2:00 A.M. the first ambulances arrived. In their lights we could see what was left of our town. I looked around, and all that I knew was gone—our house, our neighbors' houses, the trees, the stores, the school, the church—all gone. The tornado was over, and we were alive. But I knew that my life had changed forever.

Exercises

Comprehension

C. Answer the following questions about the feature story, "Tornado."

1. What happened?
2. Who is the story about?
3. When did it happen?
4. Where did it happen?

D. As a class make a timeline like the following one. Make a list of what happened in the beginning, middle, and end of the story.

BEGINNING	MIDDLE	END
1.	1.	1.
2.	2.	2.
3.	3.	3.
4.	4.	4.

E. Finish the following sentences about the story.

1. Before the family went to bed, they were a little nervous because

   _____.

2. After John went to bed, he saw _____ and he
   heard _____.

3. He never went to the basement during the storm because

   _____.

4. The tornado was over in about _____.
5. At first, John couldn't move because _____.
6. When he opened his eyes, he saw _____ and
   he heard _____.
7. The miracle was that _____.
8. The town looked completely different because _____.
9. After the tornado, John knew that _____.

Vocabulary

F. Fill in the blanks with words from the following list.

lightning	severe	thunderstorms
miracle	whistle	jet

1. Some people don't like _____, but I love the loud
   noise and the rain.
2. During the storm, there was bright _____ in the
   sky, and then everything was dark.
3. I flew in a large _____ from New York to Hong
   Kong.
4. The family had a terrible car accident, but no one was hurt. It
   was a _____ they were all OK.
5. The storm was _____. Many trees fell down, and
   we had no electricity for 30 minutes.
6. The engineer on the train blows the _____ to warn
   everyone that the train is coming.

G. Choose a word from column A and a word from column B and make a sentence. Try to make sentences that are different from those in the story.

Example: *The roaring fire burned the whole garage* .

Column A	Column B	
bright	rain	storm
roaring	fire	flash of light
severe	wind	lion
whistling	sun	day
warm	light	sky
strange	sound	tornado
	noise	jet

Listening

H. Books closed. You will hear a radio weather report for the week. After you listen to the report twice, answer the true/false questions about it.

> And now for the five-day weather forecast. It will be sunny and warm today. The high temperature will be 82 degrees, and the winds will be from the south at 6 to 12 miles per hour. Tonight, the low temperature will be 59 degrees, and it will become cloudy with showers and thunderstorms. Some of these thunderstorms could be severe, with high winds. We'll give you more information later.
>
> It looks like a very rainy week ahead. There is a possibility for rain or light showers nearly every day. Temperatures will be in the lower seventies.
>
> Now write *T* for true and *F* for false to the following questions as your teacher reads them aloud. Then open your book to check your answers.

___ 1. Today is a good day for a picnic.
___ 2. There's no wind today.
___ 3. We should listen to the radio later for more information on the thunderstorms.
___ 4. The thunderstorms tonight might not be severe.
___ 5. I won't need to take my umbrella to work this week.
___ 6. Temperatures will be very cold this week.

Conversation

I. In the story "Tornado," John says that his life has changed. In groups of three, discuss the following questions. Then share your answers with the whole class.

1. In what way do you think John's life has changed?
2. Do you think the changes are good or bad?
3. Was there a time when your whole life changed? Tell the people in your group about that time.

Writing

J. Bring some interesting pictures from the newspaper to your next class. Then with a partner, write four questions for each picture (who, what, when, and where).

K. Write a story about one of the two pictures (*See exercise J.*) Use the questions you wrote in exercise J to get started. After writing, exchange papers and compare.

L. (You will need the comics page from several newspapers. Black out the dialogue in the comics.) Divide into groups. Each group should select a comic strip to use. Then write a new dialogue for each comic strip. You may want to use "Peanuts," "Dennis the Menace," "Calvin and Hobbes," or "Blondie."

Skill Builder

M. The following is a TV guide from the feature section of a newspaper. Discuss the guide, then answer the questions that follow.

	MONDAY, MAY 22					
	6:00	**6:30**	**7:00**	**7:30**	**8:00**	**8:30**
3 **WBC**	Local News	Family Fun	Movie: A Day to Remember			
7 **WETA**	Local News	The Game Show	Al and Ernie	Science: The Wonders of the World		
11 **WBSC**	News Around the World		Cartoon Classics	Adventure: Trip to Alaska		
9 **The Movie Station**	A Look at Movies: Kung Fu Classic					

Answer the following questions using the TV guide.

1. It's 6:00, and you want to watch the local news. Which stations can you watch?

2. Which station has the most news?

3. What is on channel 7 at 7:30?

4. It's 7:00, and you want to watch a movie. Which movies can you choose?

5. What is on channel 11 at 7:30?

Make up your own questions about the TV guide, and ask a partner the questions.

More Reading

N. The feature section of the newspaper often includes fun reading, like the following quiz, puzzle, and horoscope. Try to find these features in the newspapers you brought to class. Then read and enjoy the following features. Discuss new words as you read.

QUIZ
FUN WITH FACTS
Score one point for each correct answer at level 1, two points at level 2, and three points at level 3.

Level 1
    (a) Who is the president of the U.S.?
    (b) What is the president's political party?
    (c) Who is the vice-president?

Level 2
    (a) Who is the governor of the state where you live?
    (b) What is the capital city of the state where you live?
    (c) What's the biggest city in your state?

Level 3
    (a) Who is the mayor of the city/town where you live?
    (b) Who is the head of the school you attend?
    (c) What's the population of your city or town?

Scoring
    18 points: excellent
    15–17 points: great
    10–14 points: very good
    4–9 points: good
    1–3 points: OK (read the newspaper more often.)

Crossword

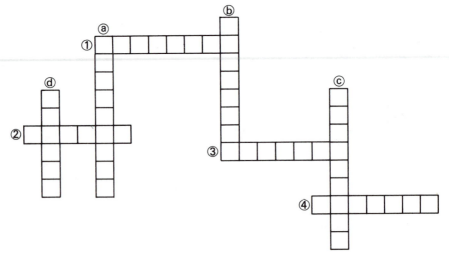

Across

1. the title of a newspaper story
2. These will make you laugh.
3. part of a newspaper
4. If you are looking for a used car, try the _____.

Down

a. A _____ tells about your future.
b. _____ are interesting stories about people.
c. The _____ is where the most important news stories are.
d. You can read about athletes in the _____ page.

Words to choose from:

features
want ads
headline
section
front page
sports page
horoscope
comics

Horoscope

A Look at the Stars
Find your horoscope from the following and read it. Then answer these questions with a partner or with a small group of classmates.

1. Do you believe your horoscope?
2. What does it mean for you?

Capricorn (Dec. 22–Jan. 20): You are not ready to make big decisions now. Wait as long as possible to decide important things.

Aquarius (Jan. 21–Feb. 19): You may want to cancel travel plans and stay home for a while. Home will make you happy.

Pisces (Feb. 20–March 20): Try not to be angry or upset, even though someone is making you worry about money.

Aries (March 21–April 20): You may be ready to make a big decision. Will it be about work or love?

Taurus (April 21–May 21): Don't believe someone who tells you that a friendship is ready to end. Trust and enjoy your friendships.

Gemini (May 22–June 21): You will have good luck with money. But be careful, and plan carefully.

Cancer (June 22–July 23): Love is in the air. It's time to end an old relationship and start a new one.

Leo (July 24–Aug. 23): The past months have been difficult, but they are behind you now. Life will be easier soon.

Virgo (Aug. 24–Sept. 23): Soon you will be rich. Will it be in love or money?

Libra (Sept. 24–Oct. 23): If people at work are making you nervous, don't worry. All will be quieter soon.

Scorpio (Oct. 24–Nov. 22): You feel playful and lighthearted. Don't forget to pay attention to your studies, too!

Sagittarius (Nov. 23–Dec. 21): You like to begin new things. What will it be this month?

Extras

O. Use the following books to learn more about tornados.

1. Branley, Franklyn M. *Tornado Alert*. Thomas Y. Cromwell Co., 1988.
2. Fradin, Dennis Brindell. *Disaster! Tornado!* Children's Press, 1982. (Also—*Disaster! Hurricane!* and *Disaster! Earthquake!*)
3. Ruckman, Ivy. *Night of the Twisters*. Thomas Y. Cromwell Co., 1984.
4. Simon, Seymour. *Storms*. Morrow Junior Books, 1989.